Youngblood was in jail and he didn't have a fix.

He sat on the edge of his bunk, waiting for the pain. Waiting for the running nose, the cramps, the nausea, the diarrhea, and finally the convulsions that could lead to insanity.

His stomach cramped some and he bent over, gritting his teeth, waiting for the full force to hit. Instead, the cramping eased and he sat up, puzzled. Again he had that uncanny feeling of something or someone standing close to him—like in the shooting gallery the week before. There was a Presence in the cell that he sensed rather than saw. It was a warm glow, a sensation that he could feel hovering around his skin, like it was all over him and inside him too. . . .

. . . Youngblood had gotten his fix—from a Source he didn't know existed!

THE END OF
YOUNGBLOOD JOHNSON

AARON (YOUNGBLOOD) JOHNSON

As Told To
JAMIE BUCKINGHAM

SPIRE

Published by Fleming H. Revell
a division of Baker Book House Company
P.O. Box 6287, Grand Rapids, MI 49516-6287

New Spire edition published 1995

Printed in the United States of America

Library of Congress Catalog Number: 72-10240
ISBN 0-8007-8625-4

The selection from *God's Trombones* by James Weldon Johnson,
copyright 1927 by The Viking Press, Inc., renewed 1955 by Grace Nail
Johnson, is reprinted by permission of The Viking Press, Inc.

The selection from "We Real Cool" is from *The World Of Gwendolyn
Brooks* by Gwendolyn Brooks, copyright © 1959 by Gwendolyn Brooks
and used by permission.

The excerpt from pp. 26–27 "There goes number seven . . . is got ekual
rights," from *Uncle Tom's Children* by Richard Wright, copyright 1936 by
Richard Wright, renewed 1964 by Ellen Wright, is reprinted by
permission of Harper & Row Publishers, Inc.

The selections from *The Autobiography of Malcolm X* are reprinted by
permission of Grove Press, Inc. Copyright © 1964 by Malcolm X and
Alex Haley. Copyright © 1965 by Alex Haley and Betty Shabazz.

The selection from "Monkey In My Mind," is from *The Complete Poems
of Paul Laurence Dunbar* by Paul Laurence Dunbar, published by Dodd,
Mead & Company and used by permission.

For Debbie

FAIR WARNING TO THE READER

SUNDAY morning. I was in New York to interview Aaron Johnson, former heroin addict, Mafia agent, pimp, for a story for *Guideposts* magazine. Now a dynamic young black preacher, Aaron was scheduled to speak that morning in a large Harlem church.

I hailed a cab in front of my Times Square hotel, but when the driver heard where I wanted to go he shook his head. "You gotta be kiddin'. Even on Sunday morning I don't drive up there." A second cab took me as far as 96th Street where I hailed a third. This driver, a black, agreed, but only after he deliberately rolled up the windows and locked the doors.

At the end of Central Park, 110th Street at Lenox Avenue, we crossed the invisible line into Harlem. It's a rectangle in shape, about two and a half miles long and a mile wide. Packed into that concrete cage are more than a million blacks—at least 100,000 of whom are heroin addicts.

It's hard to realize the crowded conditions unless you imagine, as someone has said, the entire population of the United States crammed into the five boroughs that make up metropolitan New York. And even then, the city would not be as crowded as Harlem is today.

7

It's the worst ghetto in the United States. People live in rat-infested, vermin-infested walk-ups piled ten high over garbage-strewn sidewalks. Occasionaly residents are awakened by screams in the middle of the night as some mother discovers her baby gnawed to death by rats.

Half the children born in Harlem are bastards. This produces a matriarchal society in the slum culture, with women not only raising their fatherless children, but owning many of the businesses (from night clubs to funeral parlors and churches). With the mother away at work the children turn to the streets—and in the streets they meet a new kind of hero. The hustler.

Four years before I had stepped into my first "foreign" culture as a writer. At that time I was a Southern Baptist pastor who had spent most of his life in small towns in South Carolina and Florida. No one could have been further removed from the life-style of the Brooklyn-Puerto Rican ghetto than I was when I walked in with Nicky Cruz to write *Run Baby Run.* Yet I soon learned that my basic unfamiliarity with the setting, the language and the people gave me advantages as an observer that a more sophisticated person might have lacked (simply because I remained horrified most of the time).

I began to dream of doing the same thing some day with a black man. But could I? The goal seemed impossible. The late Malcolm X declared that no white devil could ever capture the soul of a black man on paper. Nikki Giovanni said essentially the same: "I really hope no white person ever has cause to write about me because they never understand. ..."

So I tucked away the dream as one that would

probably always remain just out of reach of my white fingertips.

Then *Guideposts* gave me the Aaron Johnson assignment. Tall, elegantly dressed, his handsome light-brown face glowed with the joy of God as he spoke. It was hard to believe what this man had been. A gang leader who savagely cut off a boy's hand with a fire ax. An addict who one day drove a gold Cadillac and the next was vomiting on himself in a stinking jail cell. A Mafia agent who made a living selling heroin to children.

Even if I could believe it, could I write it? As a white southerner could I capture the unbelievable violence of this black jungle? Could I sympathize with a life-style whose basic morality was "don't get caught"? Could I identify with an entire city where everyone wore a mask, where all talk was double-talk, and the only safety was in anonymity? Could I grasp, with pencil on paper, the world of Harlem where the first question asked is, "What's your game?"

Yet as I grew to know and respect Aaron, this fiery young black, my dream began to take on substance. I caught an insight into his tortured life and saw things common to us all: the desire to be somebody, the desire to be loved, the desire to achieve. I began to see in Harlem not an alien culture but a microcosm of the world's pain. Aaron's blackness and Harlem's anguish only accented the problems all of us know. Sin is not more prevalent in Harlem, only easier to see; despair is not more frequent, only more obvious. And God too, when He moves against Harlem's backdrop, stands out in unmistakable glory.

For the next two years I burrowed into Aaron's soul, into that place where man is neither black nor white and, with our hearts beating as one, I wrote it as he told it to me: the horror of Youngblood's Harlem and the greatness of Aaron's God.

I knew I had no choice but to tell the story just as it happened. I knew many of my white Christian brothers would find the episodes so shocking, so sickening, they would simply put the book down and read no further. We knew some of Aaron's black militant brothers would think he had copped out. It made no difference to us. We knew the story had to be told.

When the manuscript was finished I mailed it to Aaron for his final reading. He called me long distance and paid me the highest compliment I've ever been paid as a writer: "You write like a black man."

One afternoon, some six months after we started, I had one of those incredible experiences of being in the right place at the right time which a writer usually only dreams of. Aaron and I had ridden the subway under the East River so that I could visit the small restaurant in South Brooklyn where he used to pick up his caches of heroin—a quarter million dollars' worth at a time. As we stood on the sidewalk outside the greasy little café, I heard a shout. A young black boy, perhaps 14, came flying out the door. Behind him were two burly white men dressed in tattered jackets and baggy pants. "Fuzz," said Aaron softly.

As the boy turned the corner his feet slipped out from under him. The men jumped him and I caught a glint of sun on steel as the boy pulled a knife. The narcotic officers stepped back but were joined almost immediately by two uniformed patrolmen who had pulled up in a police car. The four men circled the boy like dogs around a cornered fox.

One of the cops made a move and the boy jabbed

with the knife. But another officer caught him from behind and pinned his arms to his side. The fight was over. They spread-eagled him on the sidewalk, face down, and searched him. Moments later he was hand-cuffed and stuffed in the patrol car.

I looked back at Aaron. His head was down, as though he could not bear to watch. At first I thought it was the pain of remembering. Then he looked up and in that instant I saw all the way into his soul. That unknown boy was the person Aaron was living for; his pain, his fear are what Aaron yearns to heal.

A lesser man would have blamed the police, the white establishment. But Aaron knew who the real enemy was. And I realized as we walked slowly back to the subway, that I was side by side with a man who would never rest until, for the sake of his black brothers and sisters, he had engaged the adversary in mortal combat and, with the help of God, overcome.

—Jamie Buckingham
Melbourne, Florida

1

THE END OF YOUNGBLOOD JOHNSON

> *Here in this huge, dark, steaming slum, hundreds of thousands of Negroes are herded together like cattle, most of them with nothing to eat and nothing to do ... In this huge cauldron, inestimable natural gifts, wisdom, love, music, science, poetry are stamped down and left to boil with the dregs of an elementally corrupted nature, and thousands upon thousands of souls are destroyed by vice and misery and degradation, obliterated, wiped out, washed from the register of the living, dehumanized.*
>
> *What has not been devoured in your dark furnace, Harlem, by marijuana, by gin, by insanity, hysteria, syphilis.*
>
> —Thomas Merton

THE END began on a Saturday night on 125th Street in Harlem. I had finished dealing out the last of my heroin to my pushers. The air was muggy; I returned to my hotel apartment and changed clothes. I hated to have on a sweaty suit.

The apartment was empty; Barbara and Toni, the two prostitutes I pimped for, had gone to a party over in Brooklyn. I walked across the thick-pile purple carpet. Purple was Barbara's color and she had selected the rug from the finest shop in Manhattan. The long white sofa faced the largest color television set money could buy. Beside the sofa was the telephone which was my basic contact with the world of the Mafia where I got the raw, uncut heroin for distribution in Harlem and Brooklyn. Along the wall was an assemblage of high quality electronic amplifiers, receivers, tape decks, speakers and stereo turntables. A Tiffany lamp, which I had picked out from an exclusive Madison Avenue shop, hung from the center of the ceiling. It could be dimmed from a rheostat mounted on the wall and it now emitted soft rays of red and orange.

I went into the bedroom. Sliding open the closet door I stood back and rubbed the side of my cheek with my knuckles, feeling the coolness of the big diamond rings against my skin. On the rack before me were more than a hundred suits and jackets, most of them tailored, some of them never worn. When money flooded in as it had for the last year, it had to be spent for something. Fancy cars, investments in business, loans to fellow pimps and pushers—still there was more money than could be spent.

I pulled out a soft suede suit. The combed leather looked like cloth. Pulling off my silk suit I tossed it in the corner. I never had particularly cared for silk, although a lot of pimps wore it exclusively. But it seemed feminine, and even though the suit had cost three bills, I knew that after this one wearing I would throw it away.

I dressed slowly, taking pains to pick the right shirt. Instead of a tie I selected a dark-orange neckerchief, first rubbing Jade East around the back of my neck. Running a cake-cutter through my medium Afro I walked back through the living room and stood for a moment looking in the mirror. "Not bad for 22 years old," I thought. And softly closed the door.

One Hundred Twenty Fifth was a blur of sound and color. I passed the Apollo Theatre and stood outside a small club, listening to the jangling music, feeling suddenly alone. Barbara and Toni were away a lot lately and Peggy, the white girl who lived with us for several months, had disappeared the week before. Charlie was dead, which was all right with me. I leaned back against the side of the building, took a deep drag on my cigarette, and closed my eyes. God, it was hot.

Suddenly I was aware of someone standing in front of me. I opened my eyes, focusing on a short little Puerto Rican fellow. He had a large Bible in his hand.

"I've been watching you, Youngblood," he said, calling me by name although I didn't recognize him. "God has His hand on your life and wants to change you."

"Mmmm-hmmmm," I said, half amused at this shabby cat's approach. "What's He gonna change me into, a solid gold Cadillac?" I turned my head and blew smoke into the noise-filled air.

The Puerto Rican was serious. He held his black Bible in front of him with one hand while he pushed his hair out of his eyes with the other. "God has spoken to me," he said. "He said to tell you He was going to change your life."

I looked at him, his faded shirt hanging out around his belt, his uncreased pants, his greasy hair. Standing more than six feet tall I towered over him. I sneered, "Man, these shoes alone cost more than all the clothes you own. I don't need anyone to change me. Beat it, bum."

"Jesus saves," he said seriously.

"Saves what?" I shot back. "Green stamps? Man,

Christianity is a white man's religion. I'm a Black Muslim."

Actually I wasn't a Muslim. Muslims don't take dope, or drink, or whore around. But when pinned down I always claimed to be one.

"Jesus came to save souls—not skins," the little Puerto Rican said.

"Listen, creep, I got things on my mind. Now shove off. You're bugging me."

I turned and moved on down the sidewalk. New York, and especially Harlem on Saturday night, is full of nuts and weirdos. Sometimes you pass people on the sidewalk who are just standing there shouting. Guys are always trying to panhandle you or preach at you. That's why I couldn't understand why this little creep got under my skin so. What right did he have to interfere in my life? I had never been to church and never picked up a Bible, and I sure wasn't going to start.

I walked ten blocks and then turned into a shooting gallery on 116th. I had been there often. It was simply an apartment on the second floor of a dingy building where an addict could give himself a fix. Getting the works from the manager I locked myself in one of the back bedrooms and slumped into a chair.

I was tired. Very tired. Harlem's rat race was killing me. My friends were being busted or dying of overdoses. Aunt Rose—I'd lived with her since I was three—had left town without telling me where she was going, humiliated over the way I was living. My habit was back up to $110 a day, a dealer's habit; all the methadone program had done was give me some breathing time before hitting the needle strong again. I was in and out of jail. Two weeks before I had been grabbed by two narc agents, pulled into an alley and beaten unconscious. Yesterday I had visited a family down the block from my hotel. Their kid had busted into a fifth-story apartment trying to steal money to buy junk. The owner had come in, seen him on the fire escape and rushed him. The kid, 13 years old, fell five floors to the sidewalk below. I could still hear that mother screaming: "You're to blame. You got him strung out! You're to blame!"

I reached into the lining of my jacket where I kept my personal supply of heroin. Three bags. Three tiny glassine bags. I knew it was too much. I remembered Barbara saying that one day I would take a deliberate overdose. All junkies do.

Purposefully I shook out the white powder into the spoon. I poured a small amount of water into it from a jar on the table and mixed it with the end of my finger. Disregarding the matches supplied by the gallery, I pulled out my gold cigarette lighter, snapped the flame and held it under the spoon. Within seconds the mixture was boiling. Picking up the medicine dropper which was fitted with a hypo needle over the glass end, I squeezed and released the rubber bulb, slowly drawing the fluid into the needle. Then, tying my belt around my upper left arm until the big vein protruded in my inner elbow, I inserted the needle into the mainline.

Immediately I felt the rush in my stomach. I knew I had killed myself. I tried to get up but could not move. Youngblood Johnson was dying.

2

I'M BLACK

The ideal black man was one who did exactly as he was told, and did it efficiently and cheerfully. "Slaves," said Frederick Douglass, "are generally expected to sing as well as to work."
—Eldridge Cleaver

I WAS 11 years old when I discovered I was different.

It was a cold winter afternoon. I had ridden the bus home after school and climbed the steps to my Aunt Rose's apartment in Brooklyn. The wind was whistling down Brevoort Place, blowing a flapping newspaper off the back of parked cars until it stuck on the iron fence that surrounded the one tree on our street. Although no longer the elegant neighborhood it had once been, this building was still one of the better ones in the black community and, regardless of the condition of the street, behind the closed doors of Aunt Rose's apartment things were always immaculate. I ran up the worn concrete steps in front of the building, gingerly touched the door handle to see if the cold metal would stick to my bare fingers, then pulled it open, ran inside and up one flight of stairs.

Uncle Arthur, who worked as a night watchman at a garage, was asleep in the bedroom. Uncle Arthur

was almost always asleep when I was awake, except
on Saturday when he sat in front of the television,
drank beer, and watched the ball games. Aunt Rose
was at work at one of her beauty salons.

I ran to the television set and flicked it on. Even
before the picture crackled and appeared I was sitting cross-legged in the middle of the floor, waiting.

It was an old Victor Mature movie and I sat fas-
cinated by the manly big actor. Aunt Rose wouldn't
let me play outside after school. She said it was a bad
neighborhood; she talked a lot about Forces that wait
out in the streets to catch little boys and turn them
into criminals and drug addicts. You couldn't see
these Forces—anyway I never had—but Aunt Rose
said they were there, just lurking and watching you.
She felt easier, she said, when I was inside.

During the commercial I ran to the mirror in the
bathroom. I wanted to see if I could make my eyebrow wrinkle like Victor Mature's.

I couldn't. I backed up and stared into the mirror,
trying to crease my forehead. I couldn't do that either.

The more I stared at myself the more I noticed
there were other things different about me too. My
skin wasn't the same color as Victor Mature's. I had
always known I was black, but I had never realized
that black was so different. The whole idea over-
whelmed me that day in Aunt Rose's spick-and-span
bathroom. I couldn't make my eyebrows go up like
Victor Mature's because he was white and I was
black. It was that simple.

During the next commercial I reached over to the
magazine rack at the end of the sofa. Leaning back,
cautious not to get my head against the flowered sofa
cushion, I began to look at the pictures. I flipped

through the pages. They were filled with white people. Not a single black face looked back at me, even in the ads. I glanced at the big calendar on the wall, the one that carried the advertisements from Sister Roberta's Funeral Parlor. All the pictures on the calendar were of whites.

I forced myself back to the television set, realizing that Roy Rogers, Davey Crockett—all my heroes— were white. Whites had families that smiled a lot. Houses with grass in front. Horses. Adventure.

That Saturday morning Aunt Rose took me to Manhattan on the subway. "What's wrong with us?" I asked, as I held her hand and walked briskly down Fifth Avenue.

"What are you talking about, boy?" she said, her high heels clicking smartly against the pavement. We were going to the supply house where she bought her Cooper's Cosmetics.

"How come all the dummies in the store windows are white?" I said, pointing. "How come the taxi drivers are white? How come there ain't no black cowboys?"

"Child, you ask too many questions," she said severely. "There's nothing wrong with us." We paused on a curb, waiting for the light to change. "It's just that your skin is darker. It's caused by the pigments. I learned all about it in beauty school."

"But how come the darker-skin folks aren't on television? How come they don't ..."

Aunt Rose jerked my hand as the light changed. "It's not the skin, Aaron! Skin makes no difference and you remember that." She lowered her voice as though unseen ears might be listening. "Haven't I told you there was Forces? It's Forces makes some get good things, some bad. I don't want to hear no more about white skin and black skin. Just mind you don't mess with the wrong kind of Forces."

But what these Forces were, and how one kind could be told from the other, Aunt Rose did not say. . . .

3

THE DARK BEHIND THE TUB

Childhood remembrances are always a drag if you're black.

—Nikki Giovanni

MY GRANDFATHER was from Turkey. He was dark, very black, and had no trouble fitting into the Negro culture of South Carolina where he picked up a common-law wife. My grandmother was the daughter of a slave, a water-carrier for the cotton pickers. She and my grandfather started out selling rags and finally saved enough money to make a down payment on some property in a shantytown called Liberty Hill in North Charleston.

My mother was 15 years old when she married an airman stationed at the Charleston Air Force Base. Home for them was Liberty Hill also; a two-room shanty of unpainted lumber, tarpaper, peeling sideboard and galvanized tin nailed over holes in the walls and roof. The shack was lighted with a kerosene lamp and heated with an open-hearth stove. The community outhouse could be found at night by the stench. In the winter when it was damp and cold lots of children died of pneumonia. In the summer everyone learned to live with the swarms of gnats and flies.

Momma was 16 when I was born. Four months later my father walked out on her. Momma tried for three years but when she was 19 she finally asked her older sister, Rose, to come down from Brooklyn and get me.

The first year I really remember is 1953. I was eight years old. It was the summer that Malcolm X was named Assistant Minister for the Black Muslims in Detroit's Temple Number One. Malcolm had cried out in his preaching. "We didn't land on Plymouth Rock, my brothers and sisters—Plymouth Rock landed on us." He had castigated his black brothers with satire: "This white man always has controlled us black people by keeping us running to him begging, 'Please lawdy, please, Mr. White Man, boss, would you push me off another crumb down from your table that's sagging with riches ....'"

But what was true of many blacks was not necessarily true of us. Economically we didn't do so badly at Aunt Rose's. She had clawed her way up through the indignities hurled at black women who wanted to go into business and was now the owner of three beauty salons in South Brooklyn with a good side business selling Cooper's Cosmetics. She promoted fashion shows, did fashion hair styling, and moved in the upper social level of the black community. Uncle Arthur was a quiet, humble man who kept to himself, working long hours at night and sleeping through most of the day. Aunt Rose bossed Uncle Arthur the same way she bossed her businesses.

She made me toe the line too. Her training was thorough and effective. One afternoon I came home from school and dropped my clothes on the floor of my bedroom before going in to watch television. That night Aunt Rose called me into my room.

"Aaron, are those your clothes?" she said, pointing to my overcoat and jacket lying on the floor.

"Yes'm," I said, wondering why she would ask such a question since I was the only kid who lived there.

"Pick them up," she said, sternly, her dark-brown face without expression.

I picked them up and started toward the closet when she stopped me. "Clothes are made to be hung up or worn," she said, her voice like crackling ice when you step on it on the sidewalk early in the morning. "I want you to remember that. Now stand still in the middle of the room and stretch your arms out."

I did as I was told and she took the crumpled clothes from me and hung them over my outstretched arms like clothes on a clothesline. Then she went to my closet and took out other clothes and draped them over my extended arms.

"Now stand there," she said, as she sat down on the edge of a chair. "Stand there until you remember so well you'll never forget again."

Her mouth was stretched taut, her black eyes were glittering at me, her false eyelashes were flickering up and down; I wished she didn't wear all that makeup. My arms were growing tired and began to ache from the strain; I felt the perspiration popping out on my face and neck. I closed my eyes and gritted my teeth, but the weight of the clothes was pulling my arms down, down.

Suddenly I felt a sharp sting on the calves of my legs. I jerked my eyes open as I forced my arms back up. Aunt Rose was still sitting on the edge of the chair, her face expressionless. But in her hand was one of my thin leather belts. "Every time you let your arms down you're going to get stung with this belt," she said.

I tried to keep my arms up but the clothes grew heavier and heavier; each time I let my arms down Aunt Rose stung me with the belt. In despair I began to cry and finally collapsed to the floor, exhausted.

"Now pick them up and put them back where they belong," she said, getting up from the chair and walking toward the kitchen. "If you're going to live in this house you're going to learn to keep it clean."

Neatness and cleanliness were drilled into me each day. Often in the evenings Aunt Rose would take me with her to fashion shows, using me as a model. She kept me looking well dressed and respectable.

Yet I never did really belong to Aunt Rose. Momma had remarried and had three other children. She wrote maybe twice a year, but I had no part in her life. I didn't belong anywhere.

Aunt Rose said that the Brooklyn schools were breeding places for crime. Therefore she sent me to a private boys' school in the Bronx. It took me an hour on the bus going, and another coming, but inside I was grateful because this way the kids at school wouldn't know I didn't have a father.

One time my brother sent me a picture of my stepfather. He was in the Air Force, too. I put the picture in my wallet and carried it every place I went, telling the other kids he was my real dad. At night I took the picture out of my wallet and put it on the little table beside my bed where I could talk to it.

"Sure do miss you, Dad, but I know you're busy flying those jets." Or, "Hey, Dad, I found this old knife in a trash can on my way home from school today. I'm going to pull it out on the bus tomorrow and scare someone."

Sometimes I would pretend that he talked back to me, but that was hard so mostly I just talked to him.

The first day of May was always Parents' Day at school. A lot of dads came with their sons on that day. I told some of my buddies that my dad was a test pilot in the Air Force. "He flies jet fighters," I said. "That's why he ain't here. He flies them planes straight up until the wings break off. Then he jumps out in his parachute. Man, he has to make a parachute jump almost every day."

That night I wrote a letter to myself from him. When I carried it to school the next day the guys looked at it and laughed. "Your old man didn't write that. If he was in the Air Force he'd write better than that."

I looked at the scrawled handwriting and shouted, "You shut up."

"You ain't nothing but a bastard," one older boy laughed. "See how light your skin is? That shows you got white blood in you. Looka me, man, I'm black all over. I'll bet your old man's a whitey and you're just afraid to let us see him."

I could feel the blood rising to my cheeks. I knew the bigger boy was baiting me, hoping I would swing at him so he could beat me up. I'd have to win this fight some other way.

"Yeah? You just don't know. My old man wrote this letter from the hospital. His plane blew up and he had to jump out with his parachute on fire. He wrote this with his left hand because his other hand was in a bandage where he tried to save his co-pilot. They done give him a medal and they gonna give him another one."

The big guy turned and stalked off, but I could tell that the little kids were impressed.

The day our summer vacation began a couple of boys from school rode the bus home with me. It was a hot June afternoon and many of the people on our block were sitting out on the steps of the apartments. I pointed to a muscular man down at the end of the block. "That's my old man," I whispered. "He's home on a visit. He gives me an allowance every day."

"Aw man, nobody's rich enough to give an allowance every day."

"Hey, who you calling a liar?" Pulling a dollar bill from my pocket, the one Aunt Rose had given me to buy a gift for my teacher on the last day of school, I threw it on the sidewalk. "See, I got money to throw away. You can have it. I've got lots more."

They snatched it up and looked at me in amazement. "You mean he gives you money every day?"

"Sure," I said grinning with pride. "In fact, I think I'll go get some more from him right now."

The kids watched, bug-eyed, as I turned and marched off down the sidewalk toward the strange man sitting on the steps. Halfway I turned around and came back. "Naw, if I get it from him now you guys will just try to take it away from me. Besides, if I wait till he comes home he'll probably give me five dollars instead of an old dollar bill."

"No kidding, man," they said. "Your old man must really be something. I wish I had a dad like him."

That afternoon we sat for a long time on the steps of the apartment while I told the kids about my dad, story after story about his wealth, bravery, generosity and love.

"What was my real father like?" I asked Aunt Rose that night after dinner.

Uncle Arthur had finished, lit his cigar, and gone into the living room to watch television before going to work. Aunt Rose was busy clearing off the table.

"I don't like to talk about him," she said, wiping off the table with a damp cloth.

"I'll bet he was a nice quiet gentleman like Uncle Arthur," I said.

"Don't you ever think that again," Aunt Rose snapped. She turned on the water in the sink with a force that let me know I'd moved into forbidden territory."I don't ever want to hear you comparing him with your Uncle Arthur. Arthur's a good man. He's never been in no trouble. He abides by the law. But that dad of yours was something else."

"What do you mean?" I prodded.

"I mean he was mean, just plain mean. Your mother was scared to death all the time he was around. When he got off from the Base he'd come home, change clothes, strap a big hunting knife on his belt and go out looking for trouble. If you jumped the wrong way he'd slice you right open."

I dried the dishes in silence, but every so often my hand moved to the knife in my pocket. *Slice you right open. I'd do that, too, anyone got in my way. They jumped wrong, I'd slice them open.* I sure wished I could have known my dad.

"Aaron you think too much," Aunt Rose would say. "You're going to get yourself in trouble doing all that thinking."

But it was dreaming more than thinking. I would often go in and sit on the floor behind my bed. Out the window, across the street from the apartment, I could see the steeple of the gray-stone church that dominated the block. I knew there was a God and that He lived in that building, but that's all I knew about Him. I would sit on the floor behind the bed, peer through the curtains and wish I could have a little cubbyhole right up in the top of that steeple. It would be just big enough for me and no one would ever know it was mine. Then I could sneak up to it anytime I wanted and sit there next to God.

Sometimes I would wonder who I really was. Maybe my aunt was my mother and my mother my aunt. Maybe I was my aunt's illegitimate son because she had been raped by a white man and that was the reason my skin wasn't dark like the other kids. If my mother really loved me like my aunt said, then how come she gave me away?

My favorite hiding place was in the bathroom. We had an old-fashioned cast-iron bathtub that sat up on individual legs with feet shaped like eagle claws. The bathtub was smaller than the niche in the wall, leaving a space just big enough for a skinny kid to crawl behind the end of the tub and fit up against the wall. Here I could sit for hours at a time, thinking, dreaming, imagining.

Aunt Rose was a strong woman. She was stronger than Uncle Arthur. Sometimes I would pretend Uncle Arthur was like my father. I would imagine him strapping a hunting knife on his belt and slapping Aunt Rose around the room when she bragged she made twice as much money as he. I hated the way Uncle Arthur just grunted and nodded. Sometimes I would go into the bathroom and crawl behind the tub and cry for him.

On Saturday when Uncle Arthur would watch baseball on television and drink beer, Aunt Rose would nag at him, complaining that he dropped cigar ashes on her carpet. She wanted him to go to dances with her, or to fashion shows, but Uncle Arthur never went anywhere except to work and occasionally down to the poolroom in the back of the bar on the corner.

In the spring of 1956 I was sitting at my desk in the schoolroom when the teacher called me to the door. "Aaron, there's someone here who wants to see you."

I had never had a visitor at school before and didn't know how to act. I walked up the aisle while 40 pairs of eyes silently followed me. Standing in the hall was a tall thin woman with soft brown skin. I knew at once who it was. My Momma.

Everything within me vibrated at once. I wanted to run to her, throw my arms around her, kiss her cheeks, her hands, her eyes. I wanted to shout: "I love you. I am yours and you are mine." But instead all I did was stand in the door, hang my head, and watch the toe of my right shoe as it made little circles on the floor.

"Hello, Aaron," she said softly, smiling what must have been the most beautiful smile in the world.

I looked back at my feet.

"You remember me?"

"Yes'm," I lied.

"We're on our way up to Buffalo and wanted to stop and see you." I thought she wanted to reach out and hug me, too, but didn't know how to do it.

"Yes'm," I said.

"Aunt Rose said we could pick you up from school and bring you back to the apartment. I want you to meet Herman, Rachael and Canda. You know who they are, don't you?"

"Yes'm," I said. Those were the names of my stepbrother and sisters.

"You'd like to meet them, wouldn't you?"

"Yes'm," I lied.

When we got back to Aunt Rose's I felt sick at my stomach, like I had been taken into a strange place and left alone. I didn't belong to Aunt Rose because

my real mother was here. I didn't belong to my
mother because she had her own family. I was just
there.

Herman was six, Rachael five and Canda about
three. My stepfather's name was Clifford. But though
I'd talked to his picture a thousand times, he was really a stranger. I didn't know what to call him. I
didn't know what to call my mother either. I couldn't
say "Momma," or "Mother." The names just stuck in
my throat. The only way I could get her attention
was to go up and shake her arm and say "Hey." Once
I even poked Herman and told him to tell his mother
I wanted to say something. Mostly I just stood back
and stared—and smiled—and tried not to cry.

That night, after dinner, Momma and Aunt Rose
sat at the table and talked. Rachael came running
into the dining room and pulled at the tablecloth,
trying to reach up and get a leftover roll.

"Stop that!" Momma said, slapping Rachael's hand.
"I told you not to pull at Aunt Rose's nice things."

I stood in the door and watched, wishing that she
loved me enough to slap my hands. But she left
things like that up to Aunt Rose, who seemed equally
confused about how to treat me in front of Momma.
As they were preparing to leave the next morning I
hid in the bathroom behind the tub.

"Where's Aaron?" Momma said.

"Aaron! Aaron!" I could hear my aunt calling me.

"Well, maybe we can see him if we come through
again," I heard Momma say. "Come on, Herman.
Help your sister down the stairs. We got to go. Your
Daddy's already in the car." Then to Aunt Rose.
"Tell Aaron we're sorry we didn't get to tell him
good-by."

I crouched low behind the tub in the darkness,
trying to muffle the sound of my sobs. I wanted to

run out and grab Mother, cling to her, hold on with my arms and legs. I wanted to scream, "Please don't leave me. Please take me with you." But I could hear their footsteps going down the stairs in the hall.

"Watch out for Rachael, Herman. We gotta look out for each other in this big city."

The darkness behind the tub swallowed me up and for the first time I broke down and cried, the sobs going unheard in the empty apartment.

That night Aunt Rose beat me for not telling my mother good-by. This time I didn't cry. It felt good to have somebody care enough to get mad.

4

THE SOVIET LORDS

*We're rough. We're tough. We black boys
don't take no stuff.*

—C. H. Fuller, Jr.

*We real cool. We
Left school. We
Lurk late. We
Strike straight. We
Sing sin. We
Thin gin. We
Jazz June. We
Die soon.*

—Gwendolyn Brooks

"HEY MAN, gimme five," Bobby laughed, holding out
his upturned right hand so I could smack it with
mine. Bobby was my new friend. His crooked white
teeth were set in lumpy, bright-pink gums which
showed when he smiled. And Bobby was nearly always smiling. His small, close-shaven head looked
squeezed in between his muscular shoulders. Bobby's
bull-like torso was flanked by thin, gangly arms that
hung nearly to his knees. His wrists stuck six inches
out from anything he wore, and the elbows of his
coat were always ripped.

I was 13 and was now allowed by Aunt Rose to ride

33

the Bergen Street bus after school to her beauty parlor
in South Brooklyn rather than going home to Brevoort
Place. Bobby, who was also a student at Boys' High,
lived on Warren Street, just a block from one of my
aunt's salons. Every afternoon we rode the same bus,
got off near my aunt's shop and met some of Bobby's
friends. For the rest of the afternoon, five, sometimes
six of us, would huddle in the downstairs hall of an
abandoned apartment, drink wine, smoke cigarettes,
and laugh. On Saturdays we would stay there all day,
maybe going out in the street to play stickball, bas-
ketball (we tossed the ball through the bottom rung
of a fire escape) or a street game called "Cocolevio
one-two-three."

Even though Bobby was bigger than I, I soon discovered that I could think twice as fast as he. Somehow he respected that and would laugh and say, "You
be the brains and I'll be the muscles. Ain't nobody
gonna hurt us as long as we stick together."

And stick together we did. I was tall and skinny,
but with Bobby always by my side, the other kids began to respect me, too. It wasn't long before a little
club of neighborhood kids had formed, and I was the
leader.

"Man, we gonna build a clubhouse over here," I
said, pointing to a vacant lot behind Aunt Rose's
beauty salon. "This is how we gonna have it. You
guys drag up those old pieces of tin. Some of you
other guys get those old milk crates. If you wanna be
a member of this club, you gotta work."

"Man, that's telling them," Bobby laughed as the
other boys scampered around gathering the junk to
build our clubhouse. "When you got brains you can
sit around and make the other guys work for you."

Before long our club swelled to 30 members and
Bobby and I were spending long hours thinking up

things to do. Aunt Rose kept me supplied with spending money, and after the club members had worked hard, I would treat them to pies and Cokes. I was already learning that money can buy both respect and loyalty.

Our club soon evolved into a gang which we called the Soviet Lords. I was the president, Bobby the vice-president and a little kid called Rat was war councillor. Rat lived in a rundown apartment three doors from my aunt's beauty salon on St. Mark's. Small and wiry with a long thin nose, his front teeth protruded in real rodent fashion. Perhaps because of this malformation of his mouth, he talked with a slight lisp, and stuttered when he got excited.

His favorite weapon was a razor blade taped to the end of a toothbrush handle. It could leave a horrible gash, as one kid at school who made the mistake of laughing at his lisp had already found out. Rat made an ideal war councillor.

Our first rumble came because we raided a vineyard. About three blocks from Bergen Street was an Italian neighborhood. One afternoon Rat came running into the clubhouse and shouted, "Hey, I s-s-seen a bunch of grapes over in W-W-Woptown."

The people over there grew grapes in their backyards which they pressed into wine. "Well, what are we waiting for," I said. "Let's go get some."

Laughing and shouting, Bobby, Rat and I raced down the street, cut through an alley and crossed over into the Italian neighborhood. "Over here," Rat shouted, pointing to a wall around a vacant lot.

We scaled the wall and before us was a big grape arbor, covered with thick green vines from which hung clusters of dark-purple grapes. The three of us dropped over the wall and began stuffing grapes into our mouths, letting the juice run down our chins and onto our shirts.

"Hey, Rat!" Bobby shouted.

Rat turned just in time to be hit full in the face with a cluster of fruit. "Just wanted to thank you for showing us these grapes," Bobby laughed, his pink gums stained purple.

"You're welcome, n-n-nigger," Rat stuttered back, grabbing a handful of grapes and smashing them against Bobby's chest.

We began to run back and forth between the vines, laughing, shouting and ripping the clusters down and throwing them at each other.

"What's going on down there?" we heard a woman call from an upstairs window.

Laughing, Bobby grabbed a big cluster of grapes and threw it up at her. They missed, but grape juice splattered over the windowsill. Her head disappeared.

I grabbed a cluster and threw it at Bobby, hitting him on the back. "Hey, whatsa yousa doing?" Bobby hollered, mimicking the Italian woman's voice. Grabbing some more grapes he threw them back. I stumbled over a vine and as I fell a whole arbor, wires, supports and vines, came down on top of me. Bobby and Rat began to pummel me with grapes as I untangled myself and regained my feet.

A back door banged open and a dark-skinned kid, several years older than us, came running out the door. "Man, I'm going to get you niggers. I'm going to cut you good."

We could see the glint of a butcher knife in his hand. We ran, scaling the wall and dropping to the sidewalk on the other side. But we heard him shouting behind us, "We're coming after you niggers."

Rat turned and shouted back, "J-J-Just you try it, w-w-wop."

Bobby grabbed him by one arm. "Man, don't stop now. If we gonna fight, let's do it when the gang's together."

The Italians did come. The next day. It was almost dark and about 30 of us were hanging around the open lot when someone came running down the street. "The wops are coming!"

"How many?" I asked.

"About 15. They all got baseball bats and clubs."

We had twice as many Soviet Lords, and most of the gang was here. "Everybody in the clubhouse," I said. "Rat and I are going to hang out on the sidewalk like we don't know anything. When they see us we'll start running and lead them past here. You guys get them."

It worked just as we planned. Rat and I waited on the corner until we were sure the Italians saw us. Then we broke and started to run, right past our clubhouse in the vacant lot. The battle was brief and bloody. The Italians were no match for the black kids who ran screaming into the fight not caring if they were hit or cut, just as long as they drew blood. When they had run back up the street we collapsed on the ground, panting and laughing.

"Howsa thata for a rumble?" Bobby laughed, his shirt stained with blood.

"Man, we're g-g-gonna j-j-jitterbug all over Brooklyn," Rat stuttered.

"Yeah, man, you tell em," the boys shouted back. "We can take over this whole city."

And that's exactly what we tried to do. In less than a month our gang had grown from 30 members to more than a hundred. We would march down the streets dressed in our blue and yellow nylon jackets. And at 13, I was the leader. I was somebody. In the midst of violence I found a weird kind of love and loyalty that bound me to the gang, and the gang to me.

We won most of our rumbles. Bobby and I would plan the strategy. Sometimes we would fight from the roofs. We had zip guns and chains, bayonets and shotguns. We took over block after block.

But I had a problem. Bobby and I both went to school in Bishop territory, at Boys' High, while most of our gang went to school in South Brooklyn. I never walked alone at school. Bobby was always beside me as a walking partner. But he couldn't stay beside me all the time and I knew that sooner or later I would be ambushed.

The first trouble came in the hallway at Boys' High. It was between classes and Bobby and I were walking together. Bobby's next class was on the first floor and mine was on the second. We parted at the stairs and I started up. Just as I reached the landing I realized something was wrong. Three guys had been following me and I was met by two others, coming down the stairs. I tried to turn and head back down but one of the guys coming up the stairs pulled a hatchet from under his jacket. I recognized him as Duke, one of the Bishops. Grinning, he advanced toward me; I could see that the blade had been honed to a razor's sharpness.

He swung, aiming for my chest. I twisted and fell back out of the way. The hatchet hit me on the shin just below the knee. At the same time the other guys began slamming me with their fists.

Bobby heard the commotion and came back up the steps. He slammed into the guys on the lower steps and they all went down in a pile. I had my hand in my pocket feeling for my switchblade when the two fellows above me broke and ran. The others had rolled to the bottom of the stairs and were beating it down the hallway. The hatchet was still on the landing and the floor was sticky with blood. Mine.

"Come on," Bobby said.

My foot squished in my shoe as I stood up. Bobby pulled up my pants, exposing the deep crimson wound in my flesh. "Man," he said, "we got to get Duke back. We got to cut him like he cut you."

One of the teachers drove me to the hospital. Bobby was allowed to go with me. The doctor who stitched me up told me I was going to be all right. "But if that hatchet had hit you any place else, you'd be in bad trouble."

After they called Aunt Rose to come for me, Bobby started in again about getting Duke. "Maybe we should forget it," I said.

"Man, we can't forget it," said Bobby. "You gotta cut the guy who cut you. It's the law of the gangs."

"Okay," I agreed. "Tomorrow's Saturday. We'll go to his place early, before he goes out."

"Now you're talking," Bobby said, laughing.

I stood up to see how well I could walk. It hurt, but I could manage. "Get Rat and four other guys and meet me at ten in the morning in front of Duke's place," I said.

"Right, Daddy-o," Bobby said. "Gimme five." He held out his hand for me to smack.

Promptly at ten in the morning we gathered in front of the tenement house off Classan Avenue where Duke lived, then made our way quietly up the stairs to the sixth floor. Each step brought shooting pains to my leg and I had to hold the banister rail to keep from falling. Bobby was behind me and behind him, in single file, were five other Soviet Lords, all in bright blue and yellow. Rat came last.

Bobby pointed out the door. Then he and the other boys slipped around the corner and waited. I knocked.

I heard Duke's voice from the inside. "Who's there?"

Lowering my voice I whispered urgently, "Hey man, I got to see you."

"Yeah? Who are you?"

"Listen man, the Lords just burned my brother and I heard how they trying to get you. If you want to hear, you better let me in. It ain't safe to stand out here."

I heard the chain lock rattling and then the bolt loosen. Just as the door cracked open, I shoved it hard. I heard the chain rip from the wall and there stood Duke, his face filled with fear.

"Hey man, what you scared of?" I laughed.

Running footsteps in the hall indicated Bobby and the gang were on their way. But Duke heard them the same time I did and bolted down the hall in the opposite direction, toward the steps that led to the roof.

Bobby passed me, shoulders down, long arms pumping. "Get him!" I shouted.

The other guys roared past like the subway express. I hobbled after them as fast as I could. By the time I reached the door that led to the roof I heard Bobby laughing and shouting. "We got him. Hold him till Aaron gets here."

I sagged against the wall as pain throbbed through my leg and up into my groin. I thought of that hatchet, glistening in the dim light of the stairwell as Duke swung at me. But I had never cut anybody. I was the gang leader and so far had kept out of the fights. But now they were waiting for me to cut someone. I fingered the knife in my pocket and was scared.

I looked down the hall. On the wall, near the steps, was a glass case, inside it a large fire ax. "Maybe I can fake him out," I thought.

I limped painfully down the hall to the apparatus. Taking the metal end of the fire hose which was coiled on the wall, I swung it against the glass and pulled out the ax. Then I made my way to the roof-top where the fellows had Duke pinned against the tar and gravel roof.

He was down on his back, with Bobby sitting on his chest and a Lord holding each limb in a spread-eagle position. I held the ax behind my back and stood over him. I could feel the blood pounding in my temples, my breath coming in short, excited gasps.

"Man, that was a mistake, running like that."

"Hey, let me go, will you?"

"Sure, soon as we return the favor. See, we hear you lost your little hatchet. Well, we found a bigger one to give you back." For the first time I brought the red-handled ax into view so he could see it. His eyes grew wide.

"No! Please, please . . ."

"Hey, listen man, we ain't going to hurt you much. No more than you hurt me. How come you're so chicken? You're beginning to sound like whitey."

I looked around at the other boys. They were staring in disbelief. They had expected me to cut him with my knife; no one dreamed that I might appear with an ax. They had no idea that I was only teasing Duke along.

"Please," Duke moaned. "Please . . ."

"Which hand swung that hatchet?" I asked Bobby.

"Seems like it was his right one," Bobby said.

"Stretch it out there," I said, nodding to Rat who was pinning his right arm to the roof. "I got a feeling they'll be calling old Duke 'Lefty' from now on."

Rat looked up, alarm in his face. "Hey, Aaron, you sure?"

Suddenly I was afraid too, with a kind of sick foreboding.

Duke's body squirmed in a frenzy. "God please ... please ... no man ... I'll do anything ... anything ...

"Pull his fingers out flat," I told Rat.

Rat jumped back. "Hey, n-n-not me. Y-Y-You might slip."

"Come on, man," I said, "I'm having a little fun. I ain't gonna do nothing."

But Rat and all the other boys were staring intently in my face, as if they saw something in my eyes I could not see. Everyone grew quiet, so quiet we could hear the sound of the traffic on the street below. Duke was weeping silently.

"Hey man," I said, trying to break the spell that gripped me so strangely—trying to get us laughing again. "Hey man, relax or I might do something crazy."

Rat was holding his arm again; Duke's fingers curled upward as though gasping for some unseen help. I slowly raised the ax above my head.

I had only been playing, teasing, trying to get out of having to cut him. But as I held the ax high over my head, something seemed to take control.

Duke's shriek split the air of the rooftop.

"H-H-Hey man, y-y-you really did it," Rat said, leaping to his feet.

The other boys had jumped up too.

"I wasn't gonna," I said. "I wasn't gonna."

'Run!" Bobby screamed. We ran five blocks before

spilling into an alley where we dropped to the pavement, heaving for breath. Only then did I see the blood soaking my trousers where the stitches had torn loose.

Crouched on the asphalt, I held my throbbing leg. I had performed an act without any conscious will of my own. I leaned over and vomited.

Duke survived, although he lost his hand. A month later, I was sitting on the fender of a car outside the school building, waiting for Bobby, when a car drove slowly down the street. I heard a backfire and at the same time felt a sharp stinging in my thigh. Looking down I saw a patch of red spread through my pant leg. I had been shot. The car roared off and I hobbled back into the building. Even though it was only a flesh wound the school nurse called an ambulance. Once again Aunt Rose had to come to the hospital in a taxi.

I knew then I had had enough school. I would leave the apartment in the morning, carrying my books, and go to Bobby's place till the rest of the kids got out of school. Because of her job it was six months before Aunt Rose knew what had happened, and by then I knew for sure that the Forces she talked about so often were real.

5

MANCHILD

> *We shall have our manhood. We shall have
> it or the earth will be leveled in our attempts
> to gain it.*
>
> —Eldridge Cleaver

THE TROUBLE was, though we were one of the biggest
gangs in Brooklyn, except for Bobby and me, most of
the Lords were still in school. There wasn't much for
Bobby and me to do but hang around his apartment
till school let out.

One day Bobby opened a drawer and showed me
some marijuana he had found that belonged to his
older brother. We clumsily rolled a cigarette and then
Bobby showed me how to smoke it.

"Don't puff it," he said, grinning and flopping down
on the floor on his back. "You take a deep drag, like
this, and hold it down as long as you can."

I lay down beside Bobby on the floor. Unlike Aunt
Rose's spotless home, Bobby's apartment was filthy.
The bare floor felt hard against my back and I looked
up at a naked light bulb in the peeling ceiling.

I took a slow drag on the crumpled cigarette and
held the smoke in my lungs. Slowly the room began
to spin, and then settled down to a nice warm place
to be. The threadbare sofa with the stained spots on

the arms didn't bug me anymore. The grimy floors and windowsills, the strong odor from the kitchen, nothing mattered. I felt I was floating on a dream..

Every morning for the next two weeks we smoked pot in Bobby's apartment. One morning his 12-year-old sister, Coreen, stayed home from school and we gave her some. After we had smoked for a while, Bobby decided he would like to jug her.

"Hey man, she's your sister."

"Naw, she ain't really my sister," he laughed, his mouth open wide. "She's my half-sister. She don't know who her old man is." He threw back his head and laughed louder, "And neither does my maw. She don't even know who my old man is."

"But man we can't jug her. She ain't even old enough yet."

"She's been jugging since she was nine," Bobby said. "I jugged her twice myself. Ain't you ever jugged nobody?"

"Sure," I lied, "but I ain't never done it with nobody's sister."

"Everybody around here's somebody's sister," Bobby said.

It was something to do. Coreen stayed home lots of mornings after that, but after a while I found myself getting tired of it. The thrill wore off—with pot and with Coreen. I began to look for others.

"I've been hearing a lot about you, boy. You and your gang."

The speaker was a slim black man, about 30 years old, dressed in an expensive suit with alligator shoes and a gold watch chain that dangled between the two pockets in his vest. We were standing on the corner of Bergen and 4th in South Brooklyn.

"We don't take no stuff off anyone," I grinned. "Ask the other gangs, they'll tell you."

"I understand the other gangs aren't the only ones afraid of you."

"You better believe it man," I said, leaning back against a parked car and drawing deeply on a cigarette. "Soviet Lords walk down the streets and mamas run out and pick up their babies."

"How'd you guys like to work for us? Part-time, of course," the dude said.

"How's that?"

"Me and my friends like to party. We don't like our parties disturbed. Know what I mean?" He winked and nodded his head.

"Sure, man, I know what you mean. You don't like the fuzz or the stick-up kids coming after you."

"I see you ain't no fool," he said. "Some of my friends wondered if the Soviet Lords might be interested in patrolling the streets for us."

"What's in it for us?"

"A little liquor and some grass for the boys."

"That's not much, man," I said, tossing my cigarette to the sidewalk and watching it roll into the gutter.

"Hey man, don't get me wrong. That's just for the boys. Since you're the president, we'd let you come to the parties. Besides, we'd make it right with you. The other cats wouldn't need to know how much."

"Listen, man, I never walk alone. I got a walkin' partner who stays with me all the time."

"Sure, I understand. Bring him along, too. That's just good business. My problem, it's these hustlers from the city."

I did know what he meant. There were all kinds of hustlers who'd come over from Manhattan and nose around until they found a party, then they'd bust in, throw a shotgun in everyone's face, and take all the loot. Who do you report it to? The police?

"You got it right, man," I said. "When's the first party?"

"Tonight," he said, giving me an address. "See you there."

The gig was held in a plush apartment heavy with liquor, women and dope. I walked the streets around the block, through the rear lots and alleys, placing the Lords in strategic spots. Then Bobby and I climbed the steps to the second-floor apartment. Everyone there was into something illegal: there were pimps, prostitutes, gamblers, burglars, numbers runners, dope pushers. "The Game," that's what it's called. In the ghetto, everyone's working a game.

Ace, the man who had hired me, introduced Bobby and me around the room. The names hinted at the game: "Slick," "Curly," "Hot Banana," "Stud," "Alley Cat," "Deacon," "Preacher," "Doc." Doc, for instance, was a real physician who had lost his license for performing abortions. He was now used by pimps to examine their prostitutes for VD, to perform abortions, and to stitch up guys who got cut and were afraid to go to a hospital. Preacher was just that: a preacher, con man and flimflam artist all in one. He had probably 50 women on a string who were giving him money. In return he would pray for them, or he might give them a good-luck charm, or anoint them with magic oil, or pass out sanctified handkerchiefs which he had blessed with special herbs from the Holy Land.

It was Ace who gave me my name. "Meet my new friend, Youngblood," he said.

"That's you?" Bobby grinned, poking me in the ribs.

"That's him," Ace said, flicking the ash off his cigar.

"He's the kind the chicks are looking for—tall, smooth and young."

I was young all right. I was only 15.

The room was filled with couples, some dancing, some in the kitchen or bedroom playing poker or shootin' craps. Anything you wanted could be found there—a trip, an orgy, a murder contract—it was all there. It was big money, big cars, pretty chicks. I was impressed.

Three nights later we were back on the job for a second party. Once again I placed the gang in the alleys and doorways to watch for cops or troublemakers. Then after promising each an extra share of grass, I went upstairs. Shortly after I arrived, one of the dudes sauntered up to me and offered to turn me on to something big. "Pills," he said. "They'll make you think fast."

So Bobby and I dropped some pills. Bobby went in the kitchen and took his with water. But the dude pulled me over to one side and gave me a glass of wine. 'That'll really jive your insides," he said.

He was right. Within moments the red and blue lights were flashing madly. I couldn't know it was the beginning of seven years of slavery.

The guys at the gigs kept me loaded with grass. Several times they paired me off with one of the chicks, but there was one girl in particular who attracted me. Her beautiful bronze face with its high cheekbones gave her the appearance of some Tahitian goddess. She turned me on just to look at her.

"Who's the flashy chick?" I asked Ace one night.

"Untouchable, man," he said, raising an eyebrow and slowly stirring his dark red drink with a finger.

"Her pimp's one of the best and he knows just how to handle her."

"Come on, Ace," I said, "at least introduce me."

"She's too old and too much for you, baby," he said.

But even as he was talking, the girl got up from her chair and came toward us. Before Ace could say anything she reached out and patted me lightly on the cheek.

I looked at Ace. He bowed politely and backed away.

Barbara and I had a drink together and sat and talked. Ace was right. She was out of my class, but I was flattered by her attention. "Maybe I'll see you again?" I said.

Little did I think how much would have happened in my life before I did.

It was a cold winter afternoon. Bobby and I had been dropping pills all day. We had taken some reds and some whites and spent most of the day slouched in a hallway of an apartment smoking grass and washing the pills down with wine.

"Let's hitch the bus over to my aunt's beauty salon," I said, as we emptied the bottle. "We can hit her for a couple of bucks."

"Man, don't she know about you? I mean, how can you get away with all this stuff without her knowing?" Bobby asked.

"What can she say? Anyway, she's too busy to care."

"I bet she does care," Bobby said.

Maybe Bobby was right. Once, a couple of weeks back, I'd come in late and found Aunt Rose on her knees in the living room. That seemed funny because

I'd never seen her pray before. What did she have to pray about? Everything was going all right for her. She didn't yell at me either, like she always did when I was late.

Then I got the idea she might be praying for me. I wanted to ask her but she never opened her eyes, just kept moving her lips and kind of moaning like something hurt her. I figured Aunt Rose knew she was losing control of me. Sometimes when people can't control you physically they try to lay mind games on you, like making you feel guilty or taking up religion. Anyhow, maybe she did care.

"Come on, man," I shouted. "Let's grab a bus." We went to the corner and waited until the Bergen Street bus stopped for the light. As it pulled away from the curb we jumped, grabbing hold of the back. I was hanging on the back end and Bobby, high on drugs, caught hold of the back left window, propping his big flat feet against the side of the bus. His rear end was poking out over the street.

The cold air stung my cheeks and eyes, making tears run down my face. But I was laughing so hard I hardly noticed. Bobby was wiggling his behind in a slow roll and shouting at people as we passed by.

"Man, you look just like a monkey," I shouted over the whistling wind.

Bobby opened his mouth and made chattering noises like one of the monkeys in the zoo. I laughed so hard I thought I was going to lose my grip and fall to the street.

Two blocks later the bus slowed to a stop at the corner of Bergen and Fourth. Since we were just a block from Aunt Rose's beauty salon on St. Mark's, I jumped off. Wiping the tears from my eyes I stepped up on the curb and looked for Bobby, but he was still on the bus. It was picking up speed now as it crossed

Fourth with Bobby still hanging on the side, looking back, laughing and shouting and wiggling his rear end.

Then I saw something he didn't see. A large delivery truck had double-parked on Bergen. I tried to shout but nothing came out. It was as if everything suddenly geared down into slow motion as I saw the bus move into the tight corridor between the curb and the double-parked truck. Bobby was grinning, his hands clutching the top of the window and his feet braced against the side of the bus. The front of the bus cleared the truck by about six inches before it caught Bobby. I saw his mouth gape open, his eyes bug, as his body slowly turned, wedged between the moving bus and the metal sides of the truck. The driver of the bus, oblivious to what was taking place, never slowed down as the mangled body slid down the side of the parked truck and dropped to the pavement.

I staggered across Fourth and grabbed Bobby up in my arms. Slowly I lowered him to the street. There was nothing to hold but the soft mush inside his leather jacket. His face, mashed out of shape, was unrecognizable. A crowd seemed to grow up out of the pavement; a man reached down and tried to hold what used to be legs against the pavement. They were twitching and jerking as the nerve impulses, short-circuited, ran wild.

Bobby died in spasms. Strange sounds kept coming from his crushed head and throat. A moment before he had been alive, laughing, shouting. Now he was a mass of twitching tissue and splintered bone. I tried to brush the blood out of his eyes but his forehead and cheekbones moved beneath the flesh. Finally the blood ceased to spurt from his body. A bright red bubble formed over his pink gums where his mouth used to be. It remained only a second, then popped. He was dead.

I felt a hand on my shoulder. "Here comes a cop, kid," someone said. "Let him handle it."

I got to my feet and pushed through the crowd. The drugs still had me moving in slow motion. All I could hear was the gurgling sounds in Bobby's chest and the sound of my own screams.

I ran, and as I ran the hallucinations became worse. Bobby was still before me, his jelly-like body spread out on the street. I kept trying to step over it but it moved ahead of me, sliding down the sidewalk. My steps were in slow motion and it seemed that as I leaped I floated, coming down each time beside Bobby's mangled body.

I don't know how far I ran but the blocks went by, five, ten, maybe fifteen until I fell to the sidewalk, gasping and retching. Feet and legs walked around me. I don't know how long I was there, crouched in the middle of the sidewalk, but I finally staggered to my feet and wandered into an alley where I collapsed against the side of a building and passed out.

It was dark when I got home and into my bedroom without being seen. Even though it was bitter cold I had stripped off nearly all my blood-soaked clothes and thrown them in a trash barrel. My hands were still caked with Bobby's blood and it had dried under my fingernails. Aunt Rose eventually came in and found me lying across the bed. I gasped out what had happened.

"Poor child," she said. I thought for a minute she was going to put her arms around me. "Poor child."

"I got to get away," I said. "I got to get away."

"Where can you go, child? There's no place to go."

The next morning, after Aunt Rose left for work, I found my birth certificate. I creased it and creased it where my year of birth was and with a soft pencil changed the 1945 to 1943, moving my age up from sixteen to eighteen. Then I folded it again, wadded it up and stuck it in my pocket. An hour later I was in the Army Recruiting Center in Brooklyn and that afternoon I took my physical examination at Fort Dix, New Jersey. Before Aunt Rose knew anything about it, I had been sworn into the army.

6

HONG KONG GUNDI

Drugs is a drag.—Aaron Johnson

KOREA. You name. it, it was there: pot, smack, VD, clap. You didn't have to catch it, it came to you. I had headed out to get away from the Forces hassling me in Brooklyn. Yet I soon found that these Forces—man, they're all over.

I met a fellow named Cotton from Memphis, and another guy named Lewis from some place in Ohio. Both were black and both had been in Korea for six months when I arrived. We were three miles south of the demilitarized zone at an army base near Cum-chon.

"I want to tell you something," the Captain said at our first briefing. "Last week we had to send two men home who got hooked on heroin. If you're fool enough to take it, then you're fool enough to die. That's what it will do to you. It will kill you. I'm just telling you now so in case any ideas about taking it you'll know what will happen. Any questions?"

Naturally there were none. There never are. The Captain waited a minute, then dismissed us.

After chow I wandered around the camp for a while, feeling lonely and far away from home. I had never traveled farther than the Bronx and now here I was on the other side of the world. It was cold, wet, and my cigarettes tasted flat. I returned to the barracks and flopped down on my bunk. No one was there but Lewis who was sitting in the corner. He saw me come in. "Want a drink, Johnson?" He held up a bottle.

I got up and went over beside him, taking a long swig from the bottle. Wiping my mouth on the sleeve of my fatigue jacket I said, "They got any grass around here?"

"You get high?"

"Yeah, I get high. What about you?"

Cotton ambled in, slamming the metal door behind him. He walked through the deserted barracks and warmed his hands at the stove in the middle of the Quonset hut.

"Cotton," Lewis shouted. "Guess what? Johnson wants to know if we get high!"

Cotton turned and walked to where we were sitting. I could tell by his eyes that he had been taking something. Without saying anything he reached into his boot with his thumb and forefinger and extracted a little bottle full of whitish-gray powder. It had a rubber stopper in the top. He tossed it to me. I didn't think it was heroin. I had seen heroin before in little envelopes. It looked like powdered sugar. This stuff was a heavy grain material, off-white in color.

Lewis took out a cigarette and rolled it between his palms to loosen the tobacco. Then, taking his penknife, he pulled the tobacco out of the end of the cigarette, piling it neatly on his knee. Taking the small bottle from me, he pulled out the stopper with his teeth and carefully tapped the white powder into the almost empty cigarette, blending it with the remaining tobacco as he did. Replacing the tobacco from his knee he twisted the end of the cigarette to keep the mixture from falling out. Lighting it, he leaned back in his chair and took a long drag. He retained the smoke awhile, then slowly exhaled.

"Man, that's good stuff. Try some, Johnson. That's where it's at."

I took a slow drag on the cigarette, inhaling deeply and holding the smoke in my lungs as I would with a reefer. I expected it to be like marijuana with its tingling sensations. Instead I felt an immediate reaction as the drug rushed from my lungs into my bloodstream. The feeling was one of peace, and suddenly I was sleepy, drowsy. It was an immediate high like I'd never had before.

"Man," I said passing the cigarette along to Cotton, "what is that stuff? It's the greatest."

"Hong Kong Gundi," Lewis said, reaching for the cigarette from Cotton and settling back with it. "Sweet baby, Hong Kong Gundi."

Cotton and Lewis slipped off and bought more of the "sweet baby" from a secret connection in our little Korean village. They said it cost $6 a bottle and, at a couple of bucks each, the bottle lasted the three of us for the rest of the night. That was the beginning. After that I got loaded every night and sometimes would start the mornings high.

During those early months I was having horrible, recurring nightmares. The image of Bobby's mangled body floated up from somewhere and broke to the surface in my dreams. Sometimes I would wake up screaming. When I got high, though, the dreams went away.

Cotton and Lewis were the only ones that knew the connection in the village, and they wouldn't tell me who it was. I happened to stumble upon it by accident.

One Saturday night after I had been using Hong Kong Gundi for about two months, I went into the village to make a date with Kim, the Jo-San I had met the first week I was in Korea. Kim was about 15 and had been the mistress of a sergeant before he was sent home. She had come up to me on my first trip into the village and asked if I would like for her to be my girl while I was in Korea. Small, with delicate features, she hardly came up to my chest. I told her yes and had been making visits several times a week to the tiny hutch where she lived with her mother and father. They always welcomed me politely and excused themselves from the room.

That particular night Kim was not at home and I wandered down the village's main street, a twisting, narrow lane bordered by cramped cinder-block houses and tiny hutches made from plywood and tarpaper.

The children, bare-legged and wearing ragged shirts even though the weather was almost freezing, played in the street's muddy gutter and bantered with the servicemen in raucous, slangy pidgin English. Several GIs stood outside the houses talking in small groups or sat alone motionless on low stools against the dirty walls.

Glancing down a narrow alley leading off the main street I saw a door open and a yellow light spill out into the muddy street. A GI stepped out, bowed to the Mama-San in the door, and laughed. I recognized the laugh. It was Cotton.

I slipped into the shadows as he emerged from the alley. He was reaching down, slipping something into the top of his combat boot. I smiled and plunged my hands deep into my pockets. I had made a hit.

Minutes later I was standing in front of the same

door, knocking softly. The door opened and a tiny woman, old and wrinkled, stood framed in the light.

"Yes?" she said, smiling to reveal a mouth full of rotting teeth.

"Uh, I would like to buy some Hong Kong Gundi," I stammered.

She bowed and motioned me inside. "One moment, please," she said, turning and shuffling into the inner part of the strange little house. From the outside the hutch was just a door in a blank wall. Inside, however, I stood in a small, dirty patio with rooms opening off it. The patio was a playground for the children, the place where the cooking and washing was done. The rooms seemed to have some sort of oven under the floors and, as in Kim's place, everyone slept on quilts on these floors. The walls were a combination of mud and cardboard, with tin cans flattened out over the holes. Two old men were sitting in one of the open rooms silently smoking long pipes. Neither looked up. Seconds later the Mama-San came shuffling back, handing me the familiar little bottle with the white powder.

"Two dollar, please," she said, bowing again.

So that's why Cotton and Lewis didn't want me to know about their connection. I paid her, mumbled my thanks, and returned to the base.

That night when Cotton offered to share his dope, I reached into my combat boot and produced my own. "You had a good thing going, didn't you?" I said.

"Man, listen, you're heading for trouble. If the CO finds out ..."

"Come off it, man. The CO ain't going to find out about me any faster than he finds out about you."

"Well, that's not all," Cotton said, pacing back and forth in front of the stove. "You don't know what that stuff really is."

"Sure man, it's Hong Kong Gundi."

"It's more than that. It's horse, man.. Smack, It's heroin."

Would it have made a difference if Cotton and Lewis had told me earlier that Hong Kong Gundi was pure heroin? I doubt it. I was simply looking for a way out and the sweet baby was the quickest trip. Whenever Cotton or Lewis tried to warn me I was taking too much, I laughed them off.

"You trying to tell *me* about dope? I been taking dope since I was 12, man, and it ain't got to me yet."

One night I knocked on the door of the hutch and found a little dried-up Korean man in the house with the Mama-San. Mama-San said he was the source, that actually she was selling it for him. He stood to one side, bowing and smiling.

"How you using Hong Kong Gundi?" he asked with interest.

I shrugged. "I put it in my cigarette."

"Oh," he said smiling and bowing. "Let me show you better way. You want to know better way?"

"Sure, man," I said. "Show me a better way."

The old man retreated to a quilt that was spread on the floor in one of the rooms and opened a box. Inside were hundreds of hypodermic needles, the same kind I had seen in the military dispensary on the base.

"You good customer of Mama-San so I show you better way. I do you big favor."

I was already way beyond Lewis and Cotton in my consumption, but I was afraid of a needle. "No, man," I said, pulling back. "I don't want to become a junkie."

"Oh, no," he said reaching for a needle. "This not

make you junkie. Junkie put Hong Kong Gundi in vein. This only skin-popper. Same as smoking. Only quicker."

Carefully shaking the white powder into a spoon, he added water and held a match under it. In seconds the mixture began to bubble and boil as the powder dissolved in the water. He put a piece of cotton in the liquid to act as a filter and then put the point of the needle into the cotton, slowly drawing the liquid into the hypodermic.

"See," he said, reaching for my arm and pushing back my sleeve. "Junkie put needle in vein. This go in skin."

He gently pinched the fleshy part of my inner arm and quickly inserted the needle. Even before the needle was withdrawn I felt a "Whoosh" in my stomach.

"Hey, man ..." I said as I felt myself floating off the floor toward the ceiling. "Hey, man ..." I was zonked out. The old man was right. This was where it was at.

I returned to the barracks walking on air, and forgot all about Kim whom I had intended to see. Coming inside, still so spaced out I didn't know whether I was floating, swimming, or walking, I spotted Lewis and Cotton on one of the bunks playing poker. I told them what had happened.

They looked at each other and Lewis said, "Man, you gonna kill yourself."

I laughed. I was so high nothing mattered. Anyway, the old Korean had told me my dope would go four times as far this way, saving money as well as giving a bigger kick.

And he was right. The same little bottle now lasted four days and I could stay high all day and sometimes into the next. At least for a while.

One day we went on a field maneuver and had to

spend the night. I didn't have my needle and dope with me and by noon the next day I was sick. Real sick.

When we finally got back to the barracks I began to tear through my locker to see if I could find my dope. Then I remembered: I had used it all up the morning before we left and had thrown away the empty bottle. Neither Cotton nor Lewis was around and their gear was all locked up. My insides were turning wrong side out. My nose was running and my stomach cramping. I lay on my bunk doubled up and moaning.

Lewis and Cotton came in and looked at me. "Man, Johnson, you're strung out for sure."

"Can't you help me?" I begged. "Can't you go into town and get me some stuff?"

"No sir," Cotton said, shaking his head. "We ain't messing with you no more. You're bad news. You're on your own."

The heaves were becoming worse. I tried to drink water but it came right up. I stumbled into the latrine and fell to my knees, heaving and gagging until I began to throw up blood.

Scared, I stumbled back into the barracks room, out the back door toward the motor pool.

"Where you going?" Lewis shouted.

"I've got to get to town," I said desperately. "I've got to get me a jeep and get to town."

"That's crazy," Lewis said, running after me and grabbing my arm. "If they catch you without a trip ticket they'll ship you up the river."

I shook him off. Nothing mattered except another fix. I pulled the jeep up in front of the Mama-San's and staggered inside. "I'm sick," I said as she began to bow. "I've got to have some stuff right now."

"You very, very sick?" a voice asked out of the shadows.

I turned, trying to focus my eyes on who spoke. It was the old man.

"I'm sick," I groaned, holding my stomach. "I don't know what's wrong."

"Then I show you best way," he smiled.

"I don't care," I said. "Just help me."

"You good customer. I show you best way."

"Hurry up, will you," I moaned, dropping to my knees and clutching my stomach. "Please hurry."

Through glazed eyes I watched him fix the heroin, spoon, water, match, cotton and needle. But then the process changed. He took a belt from his silk jacket and wrapped it around my upper arm above the elbow. I watched the big vein in my inner elbow bulge. Expertly he injected the needle into the vein and slowly pushed the plunger.

By the time he had withdrawn the needle I felt the rush, only this time it was unlike anything I'd ever experienced before. I felt it first in my stomach, as the knots disappeared accompanied by a feeling of heat that filled my insides. Then in my head, a pleasing peace that I could almost taste. Then all over my body as I relaxed and began to float. It was like an intense but lingering sexual orgasm that extends to every nerve ending.

The Mama-San led me to a low bench and let me sit down, I dropped my head toward my knees, nodding as the liquid peace and security swept over me. It was a baptism of serenity; it made little difference at that moment that I was now a mainliner.

7

MONKEY IN MY MIND

I know why the caged bird sings, ah me,
When his wing is bruised and his bosom sore—
When he beats his bars and he would be free;
It is not a carol of joy or glee,
But a prayer that he sends from his heart's
      deep core,
But a plea, that upward to Heaven he flings—
I know why the caged bird sings!
                    —Paul Laurence Dunbar

THE MOMENT I realized I was hooked, I began to think, hope and scheme for a way to get the monkey off my back. I had sought freedom in Hong Kong Gundi but had found slavery. Even Cotton and Lewis weren't prepared for how I began to live and think— like a predatory animal prowling and scavenging for dope. I had fallen in love with the high ... the rush, the peace, the euphoria. It haunted me awake and asleep. The feeling of the rush was the most delicious, satisfying feeling the world could produce. And I knew nothing else. Hong Kong Gundi was my God— yet at the same time my executioner.

I wanted to kick. I knew it was destroying me. Yet I didn't know how. And even if I had, the craving and lust for the rush would have pulled me back in. I always felt I could kick. I conjured up plans to start tomorrow, or tonight, or after my last shot—but I never did. It was a pattern that was to be my life for the next five years. For not only was my body addicted, but my mind as well. Even my subconscious was addicted. I lived for heroin. I dreamed of heroin. Heroin was everything—my wife, my ambition, my future. Food became unimportant. Sex became unimportant. My personal safety and health were unimportant. The only thing that had meaning was getting high.

I forgot about the army. I forgot about Cotton and Lewis. I forgot about Brooklyn, Aunt Rose, Bobby. Nothing bothered me as long as I was high. I was living from one fix to another. A loner. Just me and my needle.

By the time I had been mainlining for six months my tour of duty was over. I knew that within days I was to be shipped back home. The thought left me cold with fear. If I left Korea where would I get dope? The same amount of heroin in Brooklyn would cost five times as much—for half the quality. But I would die without it. My only hope was to get an extension of my tour in Korea so I could be near my source. Then, when I kicked the habit, I could go home.

Eighth Army HQ extended my tour of duty upon request. I hoped I could kick the habit and go home, but if not I planned to get discharged in Korea and just stay close to my source of supply—forever. But instead of kicking the habit, it grew worse. Every day I awoke, staggered to the latrine, took a wake-up shot, and built fantasies about how this was the last shot I would take. But the days went on and on. The thing had total control of me.

I was sick every morning and if someone was in the latrine I would have to get up in the dark, sneak outside half-dressed in the freezing cold to take a fix.

The combination of the cold and my own nervousness
caused my hands to shake. One morning I spilled the
dope as it boiled in the spoon and had to do it all
over, with barely enough left in the bottle. Another
day a soldier came into the latrine just as I was
preparing to shoot, and I had to hide my works and
pretend I was looking for something. At times I didn't
have any water and had to find a mud puddle on the
ground. One night I woke up screaming. I had
dreamed I had used up all my dope the night before
and was going to have to face the dawn without a
shot. My daylight hours were spent scheming, making
up reasons to get into the village. At least once a
week I would go on sick call since the 15th Air Med
was on the other side of the village and I could usually break away and pick up some heroin going or
coming. My addiction had turned me into an expert
liar, so accomplished, in fact, that I was able to fool
old pros like my sergeant and even the platoon leader
who had listened to goldbricks for years. By the end
of my extension I was taking three shots a day of raw
heroin—the equivalent of three times that much if I
had been buying the garbage they sold in the States.
It was a $50-a-day habit which in Korea was only
costing me about $5.

In the 23rd month I was busted. I was rushing one
morning to get a fix and rushed too fast. Leaving my
barracks I walked through the snow to an empty
Quonset hut where I got set. I had my water ready,
my arm tied up, but I thought someone was coming
and I hurried, putting too much stuff in the spoon.
Without realizing it I took an overdose. There were
no immediate effects except the usual rush, so I had
time to clean up before leaving. Since the needle
tracks had begun to show on my arm I scoured my
skin with a toothbrush, then rubbed cocoa butter into

the marks. After I hid my works in the empty hut, I headed for breakfast.

By the time I sat down at the table I realized something was wrong. The Korean houseboy served my plate, but the minute he put it before me I went out, dropping forward, my face in the scrambled eggs.

When I woke up the medic was standing over me. I could barely see him. I nodded and went out again. The next time I woke up the CO was there too.

"Johnson, have you taken some kind of drug?" he asked.

I couldn't focus my eyes on him and when I tried to talk my head began to nod.

"He's on some kind of stuff, sir," the medic said.

"Okay, get him to his barracks," the officer ordered.

A couple of the men volunteered to half drag, half steer me back to my bunk where I sat on the side, nodding.

"Where's the stuff?" the officer said, feeling under my pillow and looking in my foot locker.

"I don't know what you're talking about," I mumbled, still trying to focus my eyes. I was so high nothing really mattered. There was no anxiety, no worry. I was riding the crest of the most beautiful wave I'd ever been on. I was right on and nothing else mattered.

The officer turned his attention to the standing locker where I kept my uniforms. My extra bottle of heroin was hidden behind one of the L-shaped metal legs at the base of this locker. As he shook the door the bottle rolled out into the middle of the floor. Sitting on the side of my bunk, I saw it roll past my feet. But I was too stoned to pick it up or even stop it with my foot. I thought I put my foot on it, but actually I reached out and kicked the officer. He turned, looked and saw the bottle.

"What's that?"

"I don't know what you're talking about," I slurred.

The medic pulled out the stopper and shook some of the powder into his hand. "Pure stuff," he said. "Let's go, Johnson."

In the guardhouse, six hours later, I began to get sick. The MPs, afraid that I might go into convulsions, had me transferred to the dispensary. But whether I was behind bars in the jail or strapped to a bed in the dispensary made no difference, I was in hell.

The pain began in the pit of my stomach like someone had reached down my throat, grabbed a fistful of my guts, and was trying to rip them out. The cramps spread to my back and legs, with great muscle spasms causing me to jerk and twist. I was lying flat on my back on the hospital bed, my arms and legs bound to the metal bars, but at times I could feel my entire body rise off the bed and remain suspended, rigid and quivering, supported only by my wrists and ankles. I screamed until I gagged, vomited and screamed even louder. Finally, in desperation, the doctor gave me a massive shot of morphine and I was able to sleep.

It took a week—seven days of hell—for the agonizing pains of withdrawal to subside. By the end of the week my body had been physically detoxified. But mentally I was still as hooked as I had ever been. After more than six months of thinking about nothing but heroin, my mind was capable of nothing else. At night, in the dispensary, I would toss fretfully in my bed dreaming about heroin. Always it was the same dream: just as I was about to shoot, it would spill, or the needle would break, or someone would come, or I couldn't get the needle to penetrate the skin of my arm. The mental agony was just as real, just as intense, as if it were really happening.

After three weeks in the dispensary I was almost insane. I knew if I didn't get out and get a fix I'd kill myself. However, the doctors had taken all my clothes except my boots, which I put on to go out to the latrine, for there was now more than six inches of snow on the ground. Late one evening another soldier was admitted to the hospital. His big army parka had been left on the bed beside mine while the nurse finished the admitting procedures. I slipped on my boots, pulled the parka over my pajamas, walked toward the latrine, and just kept going. I had no socks, no clothes except my white pajamas, no hat. The Air Med guards must have thought I was a cook from one of the other outfits. No one stopped me as I walked through the snow, out the gate and down into the village. Nothing mattered except getting another fix.

The Mama-San let me stay in her hutch. For five days I lay on the warm floor, shooting more heroin than I had ever shot before, trying to catch up on all that I had missed while I had been in the hospital. I gave the Mama-San my watch, which was the only possession I had, and promised to repay her when I got straightened out. She never questioned me, allowing me to sit around all day watching the half-naked little children running around the patio, listening to the strange language.

"Man, I ain't ever going back," I told the Mama-San. "I'm going to stay here the rest of my life and take Hong Kong Gundi. This is where it's at."

At the end of the five days I was so spaced out, I began to believe I had mistreated the medics and the MPs by escaping from the dispensary. They were nice guys. Great guys. The next day I got up, left the hutch, walked back to the base and turned myself in at the orderly room. They took me back to the hospital and put me in bed, this time in the guarded ward.

I had anticipated this, however, and had made arrangements with Kim to visit me in the hospital. She kept me supplied with Hong Kong Gundi from the Mama-San, ingeniously hidden in a pack of cigarettes which she brought every other day. Sometimes she couldn't get in and would give the cigarettes to the guards who would give them to me. The works were easy to come by in the hospital. At night I would pull the blanket up around my face and fix the works while the guards were standing talking at the end of the room. I knew I was strung out again, and I knew they were probably going to ship me home, but tomorrow never matters for a junkie, only today.

They shipped me home. My little bit of dope lasted until I got to Japan on the boat, then it ran out. From there across the Pacific I shot everything I could get my hands on. I searched the ship looking for junk. I asked the sailors (at least those who looked like they might be junkies) but no one had anything. I went to sick bay and got aspirin which I crushed and shot into my veins. I complained of toothaches and the pain medicine they gave me I crushed, melted, and shot up. I had to kick cold turkey again on the ship and it was some kind of bad. At night I couldn't sleep but would walk the decks, the salt spray blowing on me. The water hypnotized me, swishing against the sides of the ship: "There's no escape, escape, escape, escape." I wanted to take my head off and scrub it clean, but I couldn't for I was discovering you have to live with your head.

I received my medical discharge in California. Unable to find any dope, I caught a train, then traveled three days across the country drinking gin and wine to kill the pain.

I went straight to Aunt Rose's. I'd written her a few times from Korea, but I hadn't told her anything. Now I'd have to. Aunt Rose was sitting on the flowered sofa in the front room of her immaculate apartment. "Aunt Rose, I got a problem. There doesn't seem to be any cure for it."

"What kind of problem?"

I fished for words. "I'm addicted."

"Addicted? To what? What do you mean?" She sat stiffly on the edge of the sofa.

"I'm a heroin addict."

She stared up at me, chin up, shoulders back, looking suddenly small against the bright flowers. For the first time it occurred to me that Aunt Rose would someday be old.

"It's not true," she said. "It can't be true. It's like anything else—you just have to make up your mind to stop it and you can stop."

"Aunt Rose, you don't understand. I've tried to stop. I've tried for a year. I can't do it!"

"Aaron, when I brought you up here to raise you I didn't expect thanks. I didn't ask for thanks. But I didn't ask for trouble either. You've had a good upbringing. Now you've got to get hold of yourself and stop talking this way."

"That's just what I can't do, Aunt Rose! I can't get hold of myself. Something else has got hold of me, don't you see? I'm hooked."

"You're not hooked!" she cried, the street word sounding strange on her lips. "Didn't I always tell you there was Forces? It's the Forces got hold of you. They've been after you since the day you were born.

But we'll fight them, Aaron! I've fought the Forces all my life and I can go on fighting."

Then the proud jaw quivered. When she spoke next it was in a tone I'd never heard her use. "I've even prayed for you," she said softly. "Sister Neal says prayer drives off the Forces, I prayed you'd come home alive and safe, and here you are. Sister Neal, she prayed, too, and she's a churchgoing woman."

So I'd been right. That time I saw her on her knees—that was for me.

"Well go to a doctor, Aaron!"

"I been to doctors in the Army."

"Well, we'll go to another kind of doctor. I'll find a psychiatrist. You'll see! Everything's going to be all right."

"Yeah, Aunt Rose. Everything's going to be all right." But even as I said it my mind was flipping through the file of my old gang members, trying to decide which one would know where I could get some smack.

8

THE MARK
OF THE BEAST

Through the night of doubt and sorrow
Onward goes the pilgrim band,
Singing songs of expectation,
Marching to the promised land.
    —Bernard S. Ingemann

"MAN, I CAN'T believe it," Rat said as I stood in front
of a bar in South Brooklyn talking to some of the old
gang members. "You w-w-went all the way to Korea
to get away, and came home h-h-hooked?"

Like the others, Rat had grown taller. Now standing almost six feet, his skinny frame was bent forward
above his waist where his back had been broken in a
gang war after I had left. This gave even sharper
emphasis to his pointed nose and protruding, over-
lapped front teeth.

"You have to help me," I said. "I don't know how to
get stuff around here."

"Well, you came to the right dudes, baby. We all
got connections."

Now it was my turn to be astonished. "You mean
you guys are strung out, too?"

"Y-Y-You called it man," Rat said. "We're all the
same. J-J-Just like you."

"Well, where can I get some horse?" I said.

"Best place to get it is up on 102nd Street in the city," Rat said, "or in Harlem."

"Harlem?" I said. "What you know about Harlem?"

"Man, I live there now. I got me a numbers thing going that pays s-s-sweet cash."

"Listen, I don't have time to get all the way over there. Ain't there no stuff around here?"

"Come on, Youngblood baby," Rat said. "Let me take you around to a shooting gallery. It ain't much but they have good stuff. This one'll be on me, f-f-for old times' sake."

The building on Carroll Street probably once housed a respectable family and had a maid to open the door. As we approached, a big limousine glided away, driven by a huge black man. "Pusher," Rat grinned.

Outside the front door a little bald man was cleaning up a puddle of vomit. To the left of the entrance on a rickety metal chair sat a very thin Negro. The nails on his right hand were at least three inches long. Rat nodded to him and the thin man went inside.

A dog barked incessantly. At last the manager appeared, a white man with a surly manner. We followed him up the stairs. A huge, angry-looking Negro lurched down the second-floor hall at us, mumbling loudly but incoherently. Doors opened off the hall into tiny, slatternly bedrooms. The paint, at one time electric blue, was crumbling off the walls. A mangy police dog lunged out of a bedroom snarling. A fat black woman in a cotton dress pulled it back with a rope. At the end of the hall there was a knee-deep accumulation of filth—soggy old mattresses, bottles, boxes. Around us the air had the stench of vomit.

"I-I-I told you it wasn't your Aunt Rose's," Rat said.

The manager showed us to a little room on the third floor, handed Rat a small cardboard box, and went out, closing the door behind him. Rat helped me mix a $5 bag because my hands were shaking so badly. I shot it but it wasn't enough. I had to have another. "Man, this stuff ain't nothing to what I was getting in Korea," I said, finally feeling the rush and beginning to relax. "I could go down to the Mama-San and buy pure stuff for $2. Four times as much."

"Cool man," Rat said. "But you're back home now, baby. And you have to watch this stuff. Some of it's poison and some of it's been cut wrong and don't have no kick. You gotta know your pusher, man, cause a lot of these cats will try to cheat you."

At New York prices my habit was going to cost $50 a day—money which I didn't have. The only way to get it was to join the millions who play the game in the ghetto—the game of taking from others.

The first one I took from was Aunt Rose. I hated to do it, but I had to have the money and the little bit she was giving me wouldn't even buy two fixes a day. So I stole the television set out of her apartment and sold it to a fence for one-tenth of what it was worth. It gave me almost enough money to get stuff for one day.

I stayed away from home for several days after that, knowing that Aunt Rose would know what had happened. When I finally came home she asked me about the TV.

"I told you I'm hooked!" I shouted. "I've got to have stuff! If I don't have the money then I have to steal."

"I made that appointment with the psychiatrist," she said. "You promised me you'd go." She was pleading and Aunt Rose never used to plead.

The shrink's office was in a building in downtown

Manhattan. It was cluttered with books in cases with glass doors on them. His desk was piled high with books and papers and every time he tapped his pipe on the ash tray the ashes sprinkled over the top of the papers and open books.

Five days a week for four weeks I sat across from him, thinking how much horse the $500 Aunt Rose was paying would have bought. By the end of the third day I realized he was running mind games on me. Day after day we sat there playing his game while he looked at me over the top of his glasses, grunted and tapped tobacco in his pipe. At the end of the month he dismissed me and told Aunt Rose I'd be all right. That night, after Aunt Rose had left for a party and Uncle Arthur was at work, I stole the toaster, electric iron and new blender. Then I found Rat and we fenced the stuff in Harlem to buy enough dope for a wake-up shot in the morning.

It was Rat who talked me into moving to Harlem. It was a steamy hot June afternoon when we stepped off the Fifth Avenue bus at Frawley Circle on 110th Street and I realized I had crossed that magic line into the city.

We walked over to Lenox Avenue, then up past the Stephen Foster Houses to 116th Street where Rat had his apartment. I thought I had gotten used to filth in Korea, but Harlem was something else. We had to keep stepping into the street around piles of rotting garbage.

Mainly, Harlem was where everybody played the game. That evening, sitting in a bar across from the Apollo Theatre on 125th Street, Rat told me about this current one. "I started coming over here about a year ago," he said, hunched over the table sipping on a beer. "I'd see people on these wild spending sprees, like money was going out of style. I found out they'd hit the big number."

Rat licked the side of his hand near the base of his thumb, sprinkled it with salt from the shaker, then lifting his beer mug licked the salt off his hand and took a swig of beer all in one motion. "Everyone in Harlem plays the numbers, I don't mean just the hustlers, I mean floorsweepers, housewives, preachers." Rat put his hand on my arm. "Listen, man, if you want to make money, the secret isn't in playing. It's in being a numbers runner."

I looked around the bar. Behind the rail were more than a hundred framed photographs, most of them autographed, of big-name black athletes and entertainers—Joe Louis, Floyd Patterson, Sammy Davis, Jr., Willie Mays, Lena Horne. I guess it was the dream of reaching out of the ghetto that made people play, the dream of making it as these dudes had. I had known about numbers most of my life. I could remember Uncle Arthur making a bet every Monday morning before he went to bed after coming in from his night-watchman's job. Then, the next morning he would check the paper to see if he had won. He never had.

"What does a runner do?"

"Simple." Rat lit a cigarette from the end of his old one and drew in deeply. "A dude on the street wants to make a bet. He finds a runner—some have ten clients, some a thousand—and says, 'I'm putting a dollar on 355.' The runner takes the man's money and writes down his name and his number. You gotta be careful about that, seeing it's against the law. You hide the list in your tie, your coat lining, anywhere. The next day the New York Stock Exchange prints the daily sales total on the back page of the *Daily News*. The last three figures of the Stock Exchange's figures are what counts. It's called the Total Mutual Handle. Every weekday three, maybe four hundred thousand people play anywhere from a penny on up. A penny hit wins $6, a dollar wins $600. A $20 hit would mean a payoff of $12,000. Of course the chances of hitting are a thousand to one. But just one winner in a block means that the next day everybody plays. Most of my customers try to play a dollar a day. A lot of them play what they call 'combinating.' Say the number is 321. If this appears in any order in the last three numbers of the Stock Exchange total, then you hit. Some of the big money boys play what they call 'single action.' That means they choose one number, zero to nine, and bet it will be the last number in the figure."

"What about the cops?" I asked.

"Man, if you play it right the cops are on your side. In fact, I got two cops who play numbers regular. Sometimes you give them a free ride, or a little graft, you know, five or ten. No runner could last who didn't help out the cops a little bit. After all, they gotta live too."

"How much of this do you keep?" I asked.

"I do all right," Rat said, elusively. "Enough to keep myself in dope. But you see there's a lot of other guys who have their finger in it too. There are the bankers and above them are the big boys, you know, the Mafia guys. Everybody gets a cut and this way the money stays in circulation. It's good for the economy," he winked.

Rat's face grew serious and he studied the suds on the top of his mug. "See those guys over there," he said, never lifting his eyes from his beer. I glanced around and saw two men at a table in the far corner of the room.

I nodded, picking up a soggy potato chip and pressing it between two folds of a paper napkin.

"The dude with the maroon shirt is a gun from up on 145th Street. I met him last week. A runner in my turf went south, skipped town, after he made a big haul. The big guys sent this enforcer down to check him out. Two days later the papers said the runner was found dead in Atlanta of an overdose. I knew the guy. He never touched drugs."

Rat bent his elbow and drained the last of the beer in his glass. "But that doesn't happen much. Most runners are honest guys. If the word gets out he's cheating on his customers, no more business."

Out on the street Rat went on. "You know, I hate to say this, Youngblood, baby, but black people are plain superstitious. I got about a hundred customers and some of them are the weirdest freaks you could imagine. Some of them play the same number every day. Others go to the horoscopes, palm readers, witches, even the Bible. One Sunday a preacher down on 117th Street preached on 'The Mark of the Beast.' He said the Mark of the Beast was the number 666. The next day most of his church officers ran out and played 666 to win. Tuesday morning when the stock-market figure came out, guess what the last three figures were? That's right. One banker almost went broke. Some of my clients play their apartment number, phone number, laundry slips, the time of day they woke up. You can buy dream books that cost a dollar that will tell you what number any kind of dream suggests."

Rat began to giggle. "Remember 'Preacher' that you met at those gigs when the Soviet Lords was watching out? Well, he's hit it real big in numbers now. He has some kind of special magic ointment he rubs on your Bible. Then whatever page you open to, you play that number. Funny thing, he's hitting a lot. He gets a real big fee."

Numbers was just one of the games played in Harlem. I soon learned, under Rat's expert tutoring, that hustling's first law was never trust anyone outside your own close-mouthed circle—and don't be too sure of them either. Never tell anybody your business and always, always lie. That was the rule.

Money had only one purpose for me, and that was to feed the habit which was eating my insides out every minute of the day and night. I started running numbers, but it takes time to build up a clientele. To earn the rest I needed I turned to shoplifting.

Rat introduced me to some dudes known as the "Three Blind Mice" because they always wore dark glasses. Like myself they were strung out and their eyes were dilated. Most junkies wear dark glasses but these cats wore them at night too.

Rat had taken me to a gig in an apartment near 117th and Lenox Avenue. This was the corner where Malcolm X did a lot of his preaching and it was one of the most popular spots in Harlem. The gig was in full swing when we got there and Rat introduced me around.

"Meet Youngblood," Rat said. "He just got back from Korea with Uncle Sugar."

The Mice nodded and one of them pushed out a chair with his foot. I sat down and waited. "Understand from Rat you might be interested in doing some business," one of them said, cracking his knuckles loudly.

"Well, you know how it is," I said.

"And I understand you got a big appetite," one of the other dudes spoke up.

"Some cats just eat more than others," I said, smiling.

"Tell you what, Youngblood," the first guy said. "Why don't you show up at my apartment in the morning and we'll see what we can work out." He held out his hand, palm up and I laid mine against it.

The knuckle-cracker's name was Charlie, the gang's leader, and for the next week he taught me techniques of shoplifting. Many big department stores use shopping boxes with a wire handle on top and cord that wraps around the box. This way it is easy for the clerk at the cash register to see if the box has been opened or not. Charlie showed me how to take a razor blade and cut the side of such a box, making a flap which could be closed with tape so the slit was invisible. The idea was to walk into a store carrying the empty box, as though you had made a purchase at another store and were now shopping for something else. When no one was looking you would open the flap and stuff the stolen merchandise off the counter into your box. Then you would make a small purchase to allay suspicion and walk out.

Dozie, another member of the Mice, had a different but equally effective method. He would go into a store and make a $25 purchase of some appliance. The clerk would put it in a bag and give him a receipt. Dozie would leave, stash the appliance, and return with the empty bag and receipt. Picking up the same kind of appliance he would simply walk out of the store. If he were questioned he would show them the receipt and they would have to let him go. Sometimes he could pick up four or five such appliances from a single store, taking such things as clocks, radios, cameras and other resalable merchandise.

I learned that getting rid of stolen stuff in the

ghetto was no problem. Everyone was looking. Charlie told me that in some apartments, every item of furniture, every appliance, every suit or dress was stolen. The fence bought the stolen merchandise for as little as ten cents on the dollar, and then sold it at a profit while still keeping the price far below what the stores charged.

From shoplifting we moved into small-time burglary. Boosting simply didn't make enough for me to feed the craving which, like a hungry lion, roamed about in my mind demanding more and more. By this time my habit was up to $75 a day. Occasionally I would snatch a purse or wallet. But I needed more and the agony of wondering day by day whether I was going to have enough was killing me. The Mice finally agreed to turn to nighttime burglary.

The Mice located a "finder." A finder is the guy who spots good places to rob, preferably on a side street away from bright lights. Another guy cases the layout for ways to get in and the best getaway route.

There were, I learned, specialists among burglars. Some work apartments only, others houses only, others nothing but stores or warehouses; still others concentrate on safes and strongboxes. We limited our activities to stores at night. It wasn't long before I became an expert at breaking in, learning to take along an aerosol can of shaving cream and spray it into the burglar alarm cage so that even if the alarm went off, it would only sound with a dull thud through the foam.

But even though our take was high, the risk of getting caught was even higher. By this time I had already been arrested several times on "suspicion" and once on a burglary charge. I knew it was just a matter of time before they hung a real rap on me and sent me away to prison for several years. Therefore, I began looking at different games, new ways to hustle, for prison with a habit like mine would be a living hell.

9

STRUNG OUT

> "There goes number seven!"
> "Headin fer up Noth!"
> "Blazin it down the line!"
> "Lawd, Ahm goin Noth some day."
> "Me too, man."
> "They say colored folks up Noth is got
>   ekual rights."
>
> —Richard Wright

ONE NIGHT Rat ran into a problem. One of his clients thought he had given Rat a number which had won. However, Rat had marked down another number and refused to pay off. The client showed up later in the evening with a strong-arm buddy and worked Rat over until he agreed to pay. In the morning the side of his face was swollen around his eye, and his lips were so cut and puffed you couldn't even see his protruding teeth.

That same night I was uptown on 147th Street. I had gone to see a little brown-skinned girl with oriental eyes. Her mother was Chinese and her father Negro. She had long black hair and everybody called her Moonglow. Drugs had pretty much taken the place of sex in my life, but I liked to look at Moonglow and I liked to talk to her. I came out of her place about two o'clock in the morning, and as I started into the hall leading to the street somebody in the shadows behind the stairs called out to me.

"Youngblood!"

I said, "Yeah," and turned around. The first thing I saw was a gun. Then I saw the cat. I'd seen him hanging around the bars where Rat made his collections. They called him Toad because he was short, squat and had a lot of strange lumps all over his face, like warts under the skin.

He just pointed his gun at my chest and said, with a sort of desperate tone in his voice, "I don't want to have to kill you, Blood, but I gotta have some stuff. I want all your stuff."

I knew he was a junkie, and I knew how desperate a junkie gets when he's down. The hall was empty. Moonglow was in her apartment stoned. She wouldn't even wake up if he fired that gun right outside her door. There wasn't any place for me to hide. He had me.

"Man, listen. My habit's down on me and I gotta have some. I mean, I gotta have some now. I know you got a bundle and if I have to kill you I'll do it." I could see perspiration on his face, glistening off the bumpy black skin. I was still half stoned from the stuff I had taken in Moonglow's place and didn't respond very fast. Toad took a step toward me.

"Listen, nigger, I'm not scared of you and I'll kill you if I have to. I don't want to. All I want is what you got."

"Man, I ain't got nothing. I shot it all in there."

Toad's hand was shaking and he gripped the revolver with both hands. I heard the hammer click back.

"Look man, if that's all you want, go on and take it," I said, really shaking now.

"Where is it at, man? Don't pull nothing crazy 'cause this gun is loaded and I'm jerky and it might go off."

I told him where the horse was, in a cough-drop box in my coat pocket.

He reached in, got it and looked inside. "Okay, man, you stay here. This is my turf up here and I know all the alleys. So don't try, you understand, don't try nothing crazy."

As he talked he was inching his way past me, his back against the wall, so he could get between me and the door that led out on the street. I just stood still, watching him. If I held my cool he'd be gone in a second and I'd be able to walk out of there alive. He reached behind him and opened the door, then slipping the gun into his jacket pocket, he turned and ran down the street.

I felt weak, I walked out on the street. Toad had disappeared and except for a few cats slouching around in some doorways, the street was empty.

I felt bad. It was the first time anyone had drawn a gun on me and I was still scared. But most of all I was bothered that Toad had taken about three hundred dollars' worth of smack off me. I knew the word would get around and I knew I was going to have to do something about it. In Harlem you just don't let cats stick you up and let them get away with it, I knew I would have to get a gun and I knew that when dudes like the Three Blind Mice heard about it they would be expecting to hear that Toad had been killed.

With a sick feeling in my stomach I remembered Duke swinging that hatchet at me on the school stairs. Remembered Bobby: "You got to get him, man. You got to cut him like he cut you." But that's the way it was. You didn't go around letting anybody put one over. If they could do that, you didn't have any business playing the game. A cat stuck you up, everybody who wanted free drugs would come around and throw a gun on you. I didn't want to do it, but I knew I was going to have to get a gun and go after Toad.

I didn't see Rat until the next night. I saw him in a bar and grill on 117th Street and he motioned me to a table in the corner. "The word's out that Toad took you for a bundle last night. That true?"

"Man, how'd the sound get out so fast?"

Rat shrugged, running his fingers over his still swollen lips. "It's all over town."

"I got to get me a piece, baby," I said.

"Man, guns is hard to come by right now. The papers are full of the big drive they got on. Didn't you see that picture of that barge full of guns the cops was towing out to sea? If you get a piece now you'll have to pay for it."

"I ain't got a choice, man."

"I know, I know," Rat said, his eyes darting around the room. "Look man, just sit tight here. Get yourself something to eat. I'll be back in a minute."

I ordered steak and eggs and waited. Thirty minutes later Rat was back. He sat down beside me and started fingering his lips again. "H-H-Heat's off, m-m-man."

"Yeah? What do you mean?" I said, stuffing the last piece of tough meat in my mouth and washing it down with beer.

"Toad just got it."

"Man, you didn't ..." I asked, looking at Rat unbelievingly.

"N-N-Not me, man, you know better than that. Toad bragged how much he took off you and some cat tried to rob him. Toad tried to get his gun and the cat stuck him with a bayonet. Funny thing, Toad didn't have any of the stuff left, he was clean when he died."

Rat glanced around the dim room and reached in his pocket. "A dude gave this to me for you." He pulled a brown-paper package out of his coat pocket. It was a grocery sack that had been wrapped around something and held together with a rubber band. He pushed it quickly into my lap under the table.

I let it slip between my legs, then clamped it between my thighs as I scraped my plate clean. "What is it?" I asked.

"T-T-Toad's gun," Rat stuttered.

Two months later I was alone in Rat's apartment. It was early Sunday morning and I had come in late and fallen on the couch in the living room where I had gone to sleep in my clothes. I was dreaming. In the dream Aunt Rose's face faded in and out of focus before me, her black hair piled high in ringlets on top of her head. I wanted to reach out to her, but my arms wouldn't straighten out. I had tight belts around both arms and they ached where the blood was cut off, ached so bad I couldn't straighten them at the elbows. Aunt Rose kept coming and going, and each time I tried to reach out, my arms wouldn't straighten. I could hear my heart pounding and knocking inside my chest. The pounding grew louder and louder and suddenly I was awake. Light was streaming in the grubby window and someone was pounding at the door.

I rolled off the sofa onto the floor, finally got my knees under me and staggered to my feet.

"Yeah . . . yeah . . ." I mumbled as loud as I could. "I'm coming."

I released the latch on the door and pulled it open.

"Aaron Johnson?" the voice said.

I focused my eyes on two uniformed police officers, one white and the other black.

"Yeah man," I said. "What do you want?"

"Do you know a person named Dozie Adams?"

"Man, I don't know anybody this time of the day."

"Well, he says he knows you. He's part of a gang called the Three Blind Mice."

"Say, what's this all about?" I said. "I ain't done nothing wrong."

"You want to come with us?" the white officer said quietly.

"No man, I don't want to go no place. Leave me alone unless you got something on me but don't try to run no game on me."

"No game, junkie," the black officer said, drawing his service revolver. "Either you come with us peacefully or we put the cuffs on you and pull you down the stairs feet first."

"Hey man," I said, backing up. "I ain't resisting arrest."

It didn't take long at the police station for me to find out what had gone wrong. I'd forgotten what had happened the day before. Dozie and the other Mice had broken into a store and stolen some silverware and cheap furs. I had taken the silver stuff uptown to pass it off to a fence and the Mice had taken the furs. One of the furs was a real cheap piece that wasn't any good; but Dozie, who was kind of stupid and did a lot of stupid things, went around in the same neighborhood trying to sell this piece of junk. Charlie and Eddy had told him to throw it away. Instead of throwing it away he tried to sell it, and he got busted. Then he mouthed on everybody he knew. He didn't know the fence or he would have mouthed on him too.

The police told me I could get off if I would tell them who the fence was. I told them that I didn't know, that it was the first time I had ever seen the guy. They booked me on a "suspicion" charge, but I knew they had me on grand larceny, which would mean a stretch in prison. It wasn't the prison charge that worried me, it was the stark reality of having to sit in a cell right now and go cold turkey.

I hadn't had to do this since I was in the hospital in Korea, but by now my habit was much stronger, deeper entrenched. My mind went back to tales I had heard of junkies who had come off dope cold turkey in jail. One tall thin black man, Frenchy, who was a second-class pimp and numbers runner, had killed himself just two weeks before in Old Queens Prison, rather than face the pain. Word was he had taken the metal clasp from his belt buckle and punctured the arteries in his wrist and jugular vein.

I remembered O'Neal, an old-time addict that used to hang around Hamby's hamburger stand on Atlantic Avenue in Brooklyn. He had been picked up on the meatball charge of "loitering" and had to sweat out three days cold turkey. They might as well have given him the electric chair. He had taken the spoon from his dinner pail and pushed it through the wire mesh over the light bulbs in the ceiling. Breaking the bulb he managed to shake the fixture until the small bits and pieces of broken glass fell through the mesh. The next morning they found him doubled up on the wet concrete floor. The autopsy found pieces of glass in his stomach.

Some junkies were experts in smuggling dope into jail. They stuck it up the rectum in metal capsules, or swallowed a rubber prophylactic holding several spoonfuls and retrieved it in jail. But I hadn't had time for these preparations. I was put in a cell block with seventeen other men, all black and all but one of whom was an addict. Misery may love company, but not when you're kicking. I sat on the side of the bed waiting for the Forces of hell to hit. I could hear the other prisoners laughing, playing cards, talking—but by common consent they left me alone.

The pain began in my stomach. Cramps. This was intensified by my fear, a fear which surpasses all fears. The fear itself was enough to kill even without the other side effects. I tried to smoke a cigarette but even after I got it lit my nose ran until the cigarette was soggy and I had to put it out. I began to shake, violently, and even though the cell was cold, perspiration soaked my shirt and dripped on the floor.

As the night wore on the men settled down, some sleeping, their snores echoing off the walls. Others talked softly from one bunk to another. The coughing, the spitting, the intimate sounds of men locked together in the same room were magnified a thousand times. Every atom of my body rattled its fetters and screamed for a fix. I tried to get up to pace the room but my muscles refused to respond. All I could do was sit on the edge of my bunk and let my head sink lower as my hands gripped my stomach.

Then came the nausea. My stomach felt like it was turning inside out as I began to retch with violent heaves. The vomit cascaded over my pants and shoes, but I was unable to move. I was dying the kind of death that leaves you alive after it's over.

Throughout the night the heaves continued until I finally fell off the edge of the cot onto the floor. It made no difference that I was lying in my own vomit and screaming for help; every junkie in that cell had gone through a similar experience. Rather than suffer with me it was easier to simply tune me out.

By noon the next day the nausea had moved from my stomach to my bowels. I was able to make it to the slop jar for my first siege of diarrhea but from then on I didn't even try to move off my bunk. Foul and stinking, I lay shivering and shaking, more alone than I had ever been in all my life. I wished for death but it eluded me and hell was my only companion.

By the evening of the second day the pain had increased beyond what I thought I could stand. Suddenly I exploded off my cot, screaming hysterically and ran full speed, my arms thrown straight up, into the concrete wall on the other side of my cell. My chest and chin caught the full impact of the blow, knocking me back into the middle of the room. Immediately all talking in the cell ceased. I climbed to my feet and felt my eyes roll back in my head. Again I ran full speed into the wall. By this time my nose was spouting blood, my chin was torn by the sharp edge of a concrete block. One of the men started toward me.

"Hey, brother, take it easy ..." he said. But an older junkie reached out and pulled him back.

"Leave him be, man. You can't do nothing for him. That demon gonna tear him to pieces and if you get around him, it'll tear you too."

I looked wildly at the men sitting around the room. No one moved. No one talked. Every face was expressionless. Every eye on me.

I screamed again and ran to the wall where I stood, my outstretched fingers clawing at the concrete block until my nails were torn and the tips of my fingers raw and bleeding. I felt my head snap back as the convulsions began. The muscles in my back began to draw until I felt my head would be pulled back all the way to my ankles. I screamed, over and over, and then broke the grip of the muscle spasms in my back and like a crossbow that has been pulled to its greatest tension, my head flew forward, smashing my mouth against the concrete wall. Time and time again I smashed my face into the wall. I felt my front teeth break off and tasted the warm blood where the ragged edges lacerated my tongue and lips. Screaming and gasping I went into another convulsion, and fell backwards to the floor.

I felt hands on me, pulling me away from the wall. Water was doused on me, bucket after bucket until the floor was awash with water and blood.

"Now open that window," I heard a guard's voice say. "The quickest way to kill a junkie is to freeze him to death."

The window was high, out of reach without a pole and hook, but soon the February air was swirling over the floor. After the guards left, a couple of prisoners helped me to my bunk where I lay shivering and crying the rest of the night.

Early the next morning a guard came and got me. I was led to an outer office where I was given my personal belongings. I was shaking so badly I couldn't get my things in my pocket and the guard finally stuffed the paper bag in my coat pocket and shoved me out the door. Rat was in the lobby and I realized only then that he had bailed me out. He had borrowed some cat's car and had the works under the floor mat. Before we had driven a block away from the jail he helped me with a fix and moments later, sitting at a stop light with traffic all around, I shoved a needle into my arm and felt the warm rush in my stomach as I floated into the soft sweetness of a high.

The past was forgotten and everything was all right once again.

That afternoon I went back to Aunt Rose's. It had been two months since I had been home but I still had my key to her apartment and I let myself in. No one was there. I took a shower and then went into my old room and crawled up onto the middle of the bed in my shorts. It had been three hours since my last shot and my body was craving another fix.

After cooking the heroin in the spoon I sat cross-legged in the middle of the bed and drew the liquid into the eye dropper by squeezing the rubber bulb. Tying up my arm to make the vein bulge, I slowly inserted the needle into the vein. Slowly, slowly I squeezed the rubber bulb. I felt the rush, that familiar whoosh starting in my stomach and spreading like waves through my body. I began to feel drowsy. The needle, filled with crimson blood, still dangled from my arm as I sat in the middle of the bed, nodding.

Suddenly I heard a scream. Aunt Rose was standing in the open door, eyes wide with horror. Aunt Rose had never seen me high, had never seen me take drugs.

Roused from my stupor I pulled the needle from my arm and swung my legs off the side of the bed. She backed away. Groping with one arm for the door, she slammed it between us. I opened it and followed her into the living room, but she sat rocking from side to side on the sofa and would not talk to me.

That night, for the second time in my life, I heard Aunt Rose pray. All night long the moans reached me in my bedroom. "Oh, God. God. Lord Jesus!" I didn't believe in God, but it sure sounded as if Aunt Rose did. Every time I woke up I would hear her in the living room, calling out to Jesus to deliver me from bondage to the Forces.

It was more than I could take. I slipped on my clothes and walked past the dark living room to the front door. I twisted the latch; it made a horrible click. The moaning prayer stopped. I pulled the door ⟩pen. It squeaked on its hinges. She knew. She knew I was leaving.

I stepped into the hall and gently closed the door behind me. I stood listening for a moment but there was no sound from the apartment. I walked slowly down the stairs to the street. It was a long way back to Harlem.

Two days later I was back in jail. This time it was a coverall charge of "intent to purchase drugs." I had gone to Brooklyn to try to pick up some smack and walked into an ambush where the cops arrested about 20 guys in a shooting gallery on Lafayette. We were all put in a paddy wagon and hauled to Old Queens. Since my body was pretty well detoxified from my prior trip to the Tombs, I knew I could kick this time without too much trouble.

And it was there in Old Queens that I met Chicago Greene. I had been hearing about Chicago ever since I first started hustling. He had the reputation of being the finest black pickpocket in the business. He had become so well known in his home town of Chicago that whenever he was seen there in public he was arrested on any charge the law could dream up. That was the reason he left and came to New York.

I learned some other things about Chicago Greene. He had got his start as a circus clown and sleight-of-hand artist and had worked vaudeville under the name "The Great Salvador"—one of the few blacks ever to break into vaudeville. Somewhere along the line he started utilizing his sleight-of-hand artistry to pick up a few extra dollars.

"I hate hustling," he said, propped up on his bunk inhaling a cigarette. "It's not God's will for a man to hustle, but I don't know what else to do."

He spoke elegantly, pronouncing each syllable with care. He used the word God a lot, but with him it wasn't a curse word. We talked about the fine art of picking pockets. Chicago claimed he could steal a man's wristwatch right off his arm.

"A good pickpocket is like a magician," he said. "One hand distracts while the other is working. Let me show you how to lift a wallet out of a coat pocket in a subway."

He made me stand, facing him. "The closer you can get the better," he said. "Let's assume the wallet is in the man's right inner coat pocket—you find that out when you brush up against him in the crowd. With your left hand gently pinch the bottom of his jacket, pulling it away from his body."

As he talked he demonstrated. The little man barely came up to my chin. He was a grandfather-type, a type anyone would trust.

"Now I reach up with my right hand to scratch my neck," he said, "and bump you on your left shoulder. This draws your attention to your shoulder and at the same time I apologize profusely for being so clumsy. In crime as elsewhere," he chuckled, "it pays to be polite.

"Now I slip my right hand into the right side of your coat—like this—lift the wallet from your pocket and drop it—catching it with my left hand. If I time my move just as the train lurches to a stop it can be done in one motion, and the man will actually thank me for my courtesy."

Chicago sad down. "I like to carry on a conversation with my client, talking about my grandchildren or how I raised mules in Missouri as a boy. Sometimes I can get his wallet, watch, tie clasp and even his belt if the buckle is worth anything."

I sat on the side of my bunk roaring with laughter as Chicago told of a dignified man he had fleeced in Detroit whose pants fell down as the elevator jerked to a stop in the main lobby of a business building.

One of Chicago's favorite tricks was opening women's purses while still on their arms. His limber fingers could unsnap a purse in a grocery-store line, take the billfold, and snap it shut again without the woman ever knowing. "But a bus is the best place," he said. "Get up close behind her as she gets on. When she opens her purse to get carfare, lean past her and shout to the driver. 'Does this bus go to 58th Street?' Somewhere you know it doesn't go. When you've got her wallet tell the driver, 'Okay. I'll catch the next bus,' and scramble off with the billfold."

Chicago Greene leaned back on his jail cot and ground his cigarette out against the side of the wall. "Anytime you see someone in a hurry to get on a bus, pushing past people to ask the driver directions, and then see him scramble off, you can be sure he's picked some woman's purse."

"Man," I said, "I don't understand this. If you're so religious, how come you do this stuff?"

Chicago clasped his hands behind the back of his head, resting against the filthy, striped ticking of the thin pillow. He stared at the springs of the bunk above him. "I'm not religious; religious people go to church all the time. But I am a follower of Jesus Christ."

"Then how come you're in jail?"

Chicago sighed. "I'd like to blame it on a lot of things," he said softly. "I'd like to blame it on my wife who walked out on me when I became a Christian. I'd like to blame it on the cops who never would leave me me alone even when I tried to go straight, on my old buddies who wouldn't believe a man could change. But I guess really it's just me. I never was able to trust God enough to believe He would take care of me if I stopped hustling altogether."

"I don't know nothing about God," I said, "but I do know that most of the dudes I've run into who claimed to be preachers were just playing another game."

"It's a hard thing to shake the world," Chicago said, still staring straight up. "I know. I've been trying for twenty years and each time I fall back into the same old trap. I used to be pretty hard on men who called themselves preachers and drove big Cadillacs and had a flock of 'sisters' fawning over them. Now I see things a little differently. Maybe, in their own way, they're trying just as hard as I am to be better, and having no more success than I have had."

Then Chicago told me the story of Little David. Little David was the man who had first told Chicago about God back when Chicago was still The Great Salvador. Little David was some kind of traveling preacher who followed the circus around and later wound up backstage in vaudeville pulling curtain ropes and helping with the scenery. He had become an alcoholic, but he still preached Sundays in a little storefront in Southside Chicago—chewing mint all the time to freshen his breath.

Chicago paused, lit another cigarette, and slowly blew smoke into the semidark cell. It was almost time for the final bedcheck and the lights had been dimmed.

"No one believed Little David was for real," he said. "Including me. I had heard him preach about

God and Jesus and all that, but I thought it was just an excuse to pass the hat. Then something happened that changed all that—and changed me too. Little David got killed."

"What did he do," I wisecracked, "get caught with some dude's wife?"

"It was late one Sunday night," Chicago went on, ignoring me, "in his little storefront near the stockyards. Most of the people had left and I was out front talking when I heard a noise inside the mission. Next thing two kids came running out and took off down the sidewalk. I knew something was wrong so I hightailed it inside. There was Little David lying on the floor behind the wooden pulpit, his head split open and blood all over the place.

"When David was with the circus he had a knife-throwing act. He could hit a moving target at 50 feet dead center. He always wore his throwing knife on his belt and I figured that any man who tangled with him would be dead. He was that good. So I just couldn't figure how these two little kids had been able to beat him up like that.

"I got to him and picked him up, but he was dying. His head had been busted open with an iron bar. He told me the kids came in to steal the offering. He told them if they needed the offering that bad to go ahead and take it. Instead they busted him on the head." Chicago's voice had become so soft I could barely pick up the words. "When I asked why he hadn't pulled his knife, he said it was for Jesus."

I stared at Chicago Greene. "Man, that don't make no sense," I said with disgust.

Chicago Greene just shook his head. "If you'd been there and seen him dying with that smile on his face, it would make sense."

"And that was all he said?"

"He said one more thing, just before he died. He said, 'Jesus didn't have to let them do it to Him, either.'"

Then all the cell lights went out, leaving only the lights in the outside passageway. "And that's when I decided to become a Christian," Chicago said. "Right after he died."

I whistled. "That's too heavy for me," I said. I climbed up into my bunk and stretched out, wishing Chicago Greene had never brought up the subject of Little David.

10

BLACK QUEEN

> *I was dead for four hundred years. For four hundred years you have been a woman alone, bereft of her man, a manless woman. For four hundred years I was neither your man nor my own man. The white stood between us, over us, around us. The white man was your man and my man. Do not pass lightly over this truth, my Queen, for even though the fact of it has burned into the marrow of our bones and diluted our blood, we must bring it to the surface of the mind, into the realm of knowing; glue our gaze upon it and stare at it as if at a coiled serpent in a baby's playpen or the fresh flowers on a mother's grave. It is to be pondered and realized in the heart, for the heel of the white man's boot is our point of departure, our point of Resolve and Return—the bloodstained pivot of our future.*
>
> —Eldridge Cleaver

I KNEW that sooner or later I would become a pimp. All the other games were kid stuff compared to the high living of the pimp. I just didn't realize it would come the way it did, or that I would wind up with the best prostitute in all Harlem as my number one girl.

I was sitting in a booth at a favorite spot, a club on

the corner of Nostrand and Fulton near Eastern Parkway in Brooklyn. Across the table from me was Cadillac Walter, a paunchy, balding black with a Fu Manchu mustache and a diamond stickpin in his tie. Rat had introduced me to Cadillac Walter and another pimp, Soulful Sam.

Cadillac Walter was drunk and talkative. I knew from Rat and others that he was one of the most successful pimps in Harlem, a man known not only for his finesse in handling women but for his philosophical sayings. "Successful pimping requires an outright loathing for women," Walter said. "That's where the thrill is. To be a great pimp you've really got to hate your mother."

The other nodded knowingly. Soulful Sam's obvious prosperity was reflected in the clothes he wore: the finest vines and kicks, pepper silks and alpaca fronts, Halloween socks matched to his half-gaiters. I had seen his car out front, a custom Eldorado with a Rolls-Royce front mounted with Texas steer horns.

Cadillac Walter continued. "Pimping goes back to the man controlling the situation before Eve bit the apple, see, and brought him down to her level and stuck the apple in his mouth. She was rebelling against Adam's authority, see. When Adam let Eve tempt him into taking the apple, he gave up his manhood. Today, man is fighting to regain it. Pimps are the only real men left in America."

I kept my face straight. Most of the pimps I had known were more women than men, but I knew better than to express myself before these two experts in the field.

Cadillac Walter winked at one of the white girls who walked past and patted the seat beside him. She was in her early 20s with long blond hair hanging down her back. She gave the appearance of being shy, the kind who would be afraid if you sat by her on a bus—certainly not the stereotyped streetwalker. "Marcia here is one of my very best girls," he said.

Marcia smiled, bashful, and dropped her head. Cadlac Walter went on as if she were not even there. "Notice how quiet she is. You know why she's quiet? Cause I'm talking. Not because she has nothing to say. She's as smart as I am, or smarter. She has two college degrees. But she's a quiet, humble, beautiful woman because she knows her position and likes it. And because of this she is a success. Marcia only works on weekends, but when you can get a thousand dollars for a weekend, why overextend yourself?"

I looked at Marcia. I could see why she could draw a grand a weekend.

Walter nodded his head and Marcia got up and moved to another booth. He continued. "Each prostitute in my stable thinks I am God. I like it that way."

"Pimping isn't a sex game," Sam spoke for the first time. "It's a skull game. You wonder why I dress like this? Because elegance is all-important."

I looked at Soulful Sam. His wide-brimmed floppy suede hat must have cost at least a C-note, his high-heeled patent-leather boots probably twice that much. "Colorful, colorful, colorful," Sam said grinning. "I knew a cat out of Miami who wore a diamond in his teeth and a diamond in each ear. He loved stones, you dig? The secret is finding the right girls. Me and Walter, we don't have to worry about girls anymore. They come to us. They know the only kind of loving we appreciate is Mr. Green, and they bring it to us. It's a good life, Youngblood. I highly recommend it."

It was maybe a month after this conversation, at a bar on upper Fifth Avenue, that I saw a familiar face. She was, if possible, more beautiful than ever, her

body matured from the full breasts pushing against
the expensive gown to the rounded hips. She walked
directly toward me as she had the first time we met.
"Youngblood," she said, reaching out and patting my
cheek. "It's been a long time."

"Too long, Barbara," I said, flattered that she
remembered me. "How about a drink?"

She nodded, and sat down on the barstool next to
mine. I lit her cigarette, unable to take my eyes
away. Her hair was smooth and soft, falling across
her chocolate brown face to her shoulders. Her eyes,
slightly lighter in shade than her skin, twinkled when
she talked or when she wrinkled her pug nose. Her
mouth was full, moist and laughing, and her even
teeth sparkled in the dim light of the club.

"I guess you know my man was busted," she said. I
had known her "man" only as one of Harlem's super-
pimps. "I worked with him for three years," she continued, "but this time it looks like he's going to be on
ice up at Attica for a long time."

I remembered Ace talking about Barbara at the
first gigs I attended. She was known even then as one
of the classiest prostitutes in New York—now, at the
age of 26, she had the reputation as being one of the
best "out there." I could hardly believe that she was
free and probably looking for a man to pimp for her.

Barbara smiled and nodded at a handsome,
bearded young black who had just come in. "That's
Kenny," she said, turning back to the bar. "He has
four girls working for him and has been trying to pull
me ever since my man got busted. He knows I need a
man behind me for protection, but he just doesn't
turn me on."

"Hmmmm," I commented, playing it cool and letting her make her pitch.

"Now you, baby, you're something different," she

said. Reaching into the glass she pulled the olive out of her martini and slowly ate it, never letting her eyes leave my face.

It was hard to believe that she was actually making a play for me. She obviously saw something in me she liked. Maybe she didn't want to be part of a stable. I knew if I could close her I would never have to burglarize anymore.

"Let's hit a few spots," she said. "I've got a bundle so it's on me."

I knew better than to argue. This was her game and it would be foolish for me to break in with a game of my own. My usual approach to girls was to flash a few big bills, buy them some clothes and take them somewhere for drinks before the main event of the evening—which for the addict is always turning on, not sex. But Barbara was the pro and I was the novice at this game. We both knew it and rather than act big I just sat back and let her be herself. If she liked me it was because I was natural and not trying to run a game on her.

We made the rounds of the clubs. Everywhere we went she introduced me to the big people, the important people. She knew them all, the numbers dudes, the dope men, the black front men of the syndicate. She took me to an after-hours party where everyone was high on pills, and then about five in the morning we wound up at a hotel up near CCNY on 135th Street.

My body was crying for drugs. Barbara wasn't an addict, keeping herself clean for prostitution, but her pimps had always been addicts; therefore she understood when I told her I needed a fix. We stopped in a bar before going upstairs and she bought me a spoon of heroin and a spoon of cocaine for herself.

In the hotel room Barbara sat on the side of the

bed; dipping into the clear plastic bag with a match stem, she held the shiny crystalline powder under one nostril, sniffed, and then repeated the process with the other nostril. "That's a one-and-one," she said. "But for you, baby, I better take a two-and-two." Then she repeated the process.

I, too, needed something to stimulate me sexually, so I shot a speedball. The mixture of heroin and cocaine hit my bloodstream, slowing down my brain, speeding up my heart. I could feel the two drugs pulling the cells of my body apart, the closest thing an addict can feel to physical arousal. The aphrodisiac was already going to work on Barbara. I knew that, for the moment, at least, I was her man.

Sitting in a café off Times Square I chatted with Rat. Barbara had staked me with a bundle, enough to pay cash for a big car, and Rat knew a dude in the city that had one for sale. It was a year-old Cadillac, with a lavender metallic finish. "Just right for your first pimpmobile." Rat grinned as we drove it out of the parking lot.

Now, eating a noon breakfast, Rat was talking. "I guess you know the word on Barbara," he said.

"What's that?" I said, sipping my coffee.

"I mean, I guess you know what her hangup is."

"Hey man, everybody's got hangups. You and me, we got a dope problem. Barbara's probably got something else. What difference does it make?"

"L-L-Listen man," Rat said. "This is different. While you were in Korea, Barbara got busted and sent to the W-W-Women's House of Detention in Brooklyn. One of the matrons took a liking to her and turned her, if you know what I mean."

"Listen man, don't tell me she's a lesbian. I know better."

"No, baby, she's a 'bi.' She likes men and women. She makes her living off men but she gets her kicks off women."

"So?" I said, pushing back my half-eaten eggs and reaching for a cigarette.

Rat seemed puzzled that I took it so cool. "Well, I j-j-just thought you ought to know. The word is out that she has several steady chick customers over in Jersey, and I think she still plays a couple of rich dames in some of the town houses here in the city."

"Money's money," I shrugged. "Come on. Let's take that Caddy out for a spin."

Barbara and I stuck close for the first week while I picked up the terminology and technique of the pimping game. A "John" is a customer. A "trick" is the sexual act. "Out there" is the street. A "hooker" is a prostitute. As Barbara's pimp it was my job to stick close while she was out there, and in many cases to work with her to rob the John while she was tricking with him.

"There's two ways to make money in this game," she said. "One is with oddball tricks. That's taking big money from rich dudes who are weird in some way. The other cash is in the Badger Game. The man I had before you was a cat who worked this just right. Once I got the John to the hotel room my man would come busting in like a mad husband. I'd do my whimper act and tell the John we'd both be killed unless he handed over all his money."

Barbara told me which lawyers to contact in case she got busted and how to tell if she was in trouble because she had picked up some sadist. In turn, she would give me all the money she made off the street and we would spend it together.

She took me out, bought me a new wardrobe, and every night we made the rounds of the clubs. If I hadn't been sick with dope it would have been a fantastic time. But as our money began to run out Barbara indicated it was time to get back out there and begin hustling. Her usual territory was between 6th Avenue and 8th near 42nd Street. She had connections there, knew all the cops, and had some old customers who had been waiting for her to return. She took a room off 42nd Street where she turned her tricks and told me to wait on the street. She would give me the high sign when she was ready to make a big sting.

I loitered up and down the street, waiting while she tricked with an army officer. Three kinds of tricks she routinely scorned were with non-whites, boys without ties, and drunks. An hour later, a youngish-looking kid approached her.

"Are you waiting for anyone?" he asked shyly.

"Maybe."

"We could blow some grass at my place . . ."

"Listen, kid. If you want to talk business, I'm your girl. But if you're just looking for a pick-up, then go back home and sit on your steps."

The boy got the message and kept walking. Then about 1 a.m., Barbara gave me a nod and I knew she had a big one on the line.

We had spotted him when his Mercedes circled the block the first time. She waited on the corner for him to return and as the car pulled to the curb she took a step toward it. I heard the man say, "How about a date, baby," as he leaned over the seat.

"Are you looking?"

"That's right. How much will it cost me?"

"I'm expensive, Mister. I'm not a street girl full of VD, you know."

"How about 50?"

"Mister, I think you better find somebody else. It costs more to go first class."

"How much?"

"For a C-note I'll make you forget everything else that's ever happened to you."

"Let's go," he said, reaching over and opening the door.

"No thank you, friend," Barbara said smiling. "Park your car and meet me under that hotel sign right down the street. I got a room just waiting for the two of us."

I couldn't help but admire Barbara's class. I'd seen a lot of hookers out on the street and most of them looked like hookers. But Barbara had beauty and style. The man looking for a $20 trick knew better than to even approach her. Tonight, with a mink stole around her shoulders, she looked like she was waiting for a cab after the theatre.

As the Mercedes pulled away to find a parking lot, Barbara turned and sauntered down the street toward the hotel. "This is a real fish," she said as she passed me. "Go on up and get ready for the catch."

I walked before her, getting to the hotel room and hiding myself under the bed. Waiting there in the darkness I could hear my heart beating. Barbara's main clientele were professional men—and always white. She wouldn't turn a trick with a black. It was the code, not to make money off your black brothers. But I didn't trust whites and didn't know how they would react if they were trapped. I waited.

Moments later I heard the key turn in the lock and Barbara and the John came in, closing the door behind them.

Toad's gun was on the floor beside my head, although I could tell from the outset I wasn't going to need it. Barbara was giggling. "Hey man, how long you been away from home. Give me a chance to get my clothes off."

Moments later they were on the bed. Barbara helped him undress, expertly laying his pants on the floor next to my head. I reached out from under the bed and slipped the man's billfold from his pants. Barbara was right. This was going to be a real sting. I counted out nine $100 bills and some smaller ones—more than a thousand clams, not counting the hundred Barbara had collected in advance out in the hall.

Cleaning him out I started to put his billfold back, then had a second thought. I put a single one dollar bill neatly back in the wallet. He seemed like such a nice guy; he'd need the money to phone his wife to send him some more cash. I had to bite my lips to keep from laughing.

After Barbara turned her trick with the man they lay on the bed for a few minutes talking. From the muffled conversation I learned the man was in the insurance business and from Birmingham, Alabama. He had a wife and several kids and was a leader in his church and civic club. He hated blacks but had to admit that Barbara wasn't like any girl he'd ever been with before. He wanted to know where he could call her.

"Listen!" Barbara said suddenly.

I felt the bed jerk as the John sat up. "What? I don't hear anything!"

"We better clear out," Barbara said. "I don't want to get in no more trouble around here."

"What do you mean, trouble?" the John said, grabbing his clothes off the floor.

"Sometimes the cops check the rooms around here," Barbara said. She was also dressing in a hurry.

"Goshamighty!" said Alabama. "Let's get out of here!"

"You go first," Barbara said.

The John didn't argue. Without a "Good-by" or a "Thank you ma'am," he cracked the door, saw the hall was clear, and was gone.

Barbara closed the door and leaned against it, laughing. "How'd you do?" she said as I crawled out from under the bed.

"More than a grand," I said, brushing myself off and straightening my tie.

"Okay, let's get out of here."

"You afraid the John will come back?" I asked.

"Not in a thousand years, baby," she said. "Johns like that are too afraid to come back, too embarrassed to go to the cops, and too ashamed to do anything but say they lost their wallet. He won't even check it until he gets back to his hotel room."

11

TONI

Beautiful black women! The Honorable Elijah Muhammad teaches us that the black man is going around saying he wants respect; well, the black man never will get anybody's respect until he first learns to respect his own women! The black man needs today to stand up and throw off the weakness imposed upon him by the slavemaster white man!

—Malcolm X

I NEVER saw a black prostitute touched by a black man, although I knew there were many who broke the code. Whites, often from the South or segregated areas, roamed the streets of the city looking for black girls. There were many white prostitutes, but in Harlem these girls belonged to black men.

Barbara was working Times Square, the Port Authority Building, Avenue of the Americas, 42nd Street and 8th Avenue as well as Eastern Parkway across the river and Flatbush Avenue where the big money was. I would pick her up in my car after she had played the field, usually between 3 a.m. and dawn (unless she had a John who was willing to pay big for an all-night trick) and we'd drive back across the Brooklyn Bridge and up Madison Avenue to our apartment on Hamilton Terrace. Barbara liked to use these times to talk, since most of the night she had been listening. I used the time to learn. I was convinced this was what attracted Barbara to me. She liked to teach me, to groom me for my role as a pimp. Little by little I became her man, her protector, her escort, her manager.

The one thing I did not become was her lover. After the first few weeks together our love-making was discontinued by unspoken but mutual consent. What Barbara's reasons were, I didn't know; for me sex and everything else had long since ceased to matter beside the one big drive in my life—heroin.

I had quit robbing completely and was just pimping and laying up while Barbara hustled. I was buying dope by the bundle and consuming it almost as fast. And my body was deteriorating. The habit was getting me and I knew I needed help. I explained things to Barbara and then took a few days away and went home to see Aunt Rose.

It was Sunday noon when I knocked on the door of her apartment. Uncle Arthur opened the door, grunted, shouted over his shoulder, "Rose, Aaron's here," and went on into the kitchen to open a beer.

Aunt Rose looked old and—withered somehow. "Aaron!" she said. "Oh, thank God!" Uncle Arthur took his beer in the living room and switched on the television so she and I sat down in the kitchen. "We hadn't heard from you. I—I was afraid you were dead."

"Hey," I said, "look at me. See, I'm all in one piece. How you like this suit? I went downtown yesterday and paid $200 cash for it."

Aunt Rose didn't even look at the suit. "Your mother called. She wanted to know about you and I lied and told her you had a job and were busy. I been saying prayers for you every night. And you remember the Neals? They're praying too."

"The Neals?" I asked.

Aunt Rose poured me a cup of coffee and I noticed how thin her hands were. "Your cousin William married their daughter. They live in South Brooklyn near my shop. You used to play around there when you were a little boy."

"Oh, yeah," I said.

"They been praying for you a lot. Sister Neal said to tell you if you ever needed a place to come that her door was always open."

"Thanks, Aunt Rose, but that's not the kind of help I need."

"You need money. I know. The only reason you come around is when you need money."

"No, Aunt Rose. I don't need money. I got more money than I can spend. It's my habit. It's killing me. If I don't get some help I'll die."

"Aaron, I've told you all you have to do is make up your mind to quit."

"No one kicks the habit, Aunt Rose. I know a lot of guys who are always saying they're going to kick, but they never do. They go away, get cures, and come back and start shooting up again. I know guys who went to Lexington to the government hospital. The minute they stepped off the bus in Harlem after six months clean, they headed for a shooting gallery."

I stood up and began to pace the warm little room. Out the window I could see the dirty gray stone church across the street. Strange, I had been raised in this block but never had been in that church. Didn't even know what went on in there. Now folks were coming out and standing on the sidewalk talking, shaking hands. The minister was standing at the door, his long black robe shining in the Sunday sun.

"Seems like all my friends in Harlem are dying," I said. "I'm getting afraid to ask about anyone because you're always hearing, 'Oh he died.' Slinky Smith, he got his mind all burned out and mistook a police station for a liquor store and tried to hold it up with a water pistol. They shot him 14 times and the guys who saw it said Slinky died nodding, like all those bullets had given him the high he was looking for . . ."

"Stop it! Stop it!" Aunt Rose shouted. "I don't want to hear about it! I've lived a good life, a decent life. I don't want to hear these things."

"There's a push on in the city, Aunt Rose. All at once the cops are arresting everybody. I've been through that kind of hell before, and I can't go through it again. If you could get me admitted to a hospital I could get cleaned up and by then things will be back to normal."

"Do you want to go to a hospital?" Aunt Rose asked.

"I got to," I said. "If I go to jail I'll die. The hospital is my only chance right now, and I stand a better chance of getting into a good program if you make the request."

Next afternoon Aunt Rose came home with the news that Manhattan General had just started a new methadone treatment. Methadone is a Class A narcotic, as addictive as heroin, but not so damaging to the body. It was just becoming popular and Aunt Rose got me into the free city program. I had to agree to stay on the regimen for at least thirty days after I got out of the hospital, which meant returning every morning to drink a glass of orange juice and get the methadone. I knew that many junkies took the methadone and heroin as well and got a double boost, but I was determined to cut down as much as I could, get my system detoxified, and then return to my life.

The program was successful, in a way, and I cut back my habit from $100 a day to about $30 a day. I was still a junkie but was beginning to gain a little weight and feel like a man again. I returned to Barbara and our apartment on Hamilton Terrace.

Barbara was complaining that the cops in Times Square were on a push and she wanted to move over to Eastern Parkway and Flatbush for a while. We rented a brick house on Bergen Street. It was a late January afternoon and I was sitting in the back of a bar on 3rd Avenue in Brooklyn waiting for her to get back from an all-day trick up in Weschester. Bubby, the round little black who ran the bar, had stepped down the street to collect some money. I had just taken a fix in the bathroom and was nodding at a table in the rear when Bubby came running back in. He collapsed on a chair across from me. "They got Tucker," he said.

I knew Tucker. He was an old hope-to-die junkie who hung around the neighborhood panhandling. "Who got him, man?"

"Babyface," Buddy said. "Shot him in the leg."

I knew Babyface, too. Most junkies get to know the cops pretty well, especially the mean ones. And Babyface was one of the meanest. He was a maniac when it came to chasing down junkies; "germs" he called them. It seemed Babyface hated all junkies, maybe because his own brother was strung out on heroin.

"Man, what did he do?" I said, looking at Bubby who was trying to light a cigarette.

Giving up on the cigarette, Bubby pulled out a filthy handkerchief and mopped his brow. "I seen it all. I was standing in the alley when it happened. Old Tucker was sitting down there in the alley," Bubby said. "He weren't hurting nobody or nothing. He was just sitting there. Babyface came along and seen him there and asked him what he was doing. Tucker leaned over and spit on Babyface's shoes." I could see where that was his mistake—Babyface had the shiniest shoes in Brooklyn. "Babyface reached down, yanked him to his feet and told him to start running. 'Man, I ain't running and getting myself shot in no back!' Tucker said. Babyface shoved him into the garbage cans and told him to run. Tucker just fell down on the pavement. 'Take me to jail then, cause I ain't running. I'm laying right here.' Then Babyface pulled his gun, and shot him in the leg anyway. Man, I was standing in the alley when it happened. I saw it."

It was always a running battle between the cops and the junkies. Watusi, a big black cop who had a beat along 4th and Warren in Brooklyn, was the one who bugged me most. He knew Aunt Rose and ever since I had come back from Korea he made it a personal point to come up to me and jaw about how I wasn't fit to breathe the same air as her. One time he dragged me into a bathroom in the back of a bar and grill and made me take off all my clothes and searched me for heroin. When he didn't find any he opened the window and made me stand in the cold, trying to force me to name my connection. I never did and he finally let me go, but I knew he was out to get me.

The very next week after Tucker got hit I ran into Watusi over on Fourth, just a block from one of Aunt Rose's beauty salons. He had two white guys with him, both of them dressed in slouchy jackets, baggy pants and rundown shoes. Narcs. I could smell them a block away. I had a half bundle of dope in my coat pocket and knew that Watusi was going to stop me and frisk me. He always did.

I panicked, turned and started to run. They were right behind me. As I rounded the first corner I pulled the bundle from my pocket and flipped it into the open door of an apartment hall and kept going. I couldn't run the way I used to but since I no longer had the dope it didn't matter if they caught me. I slowed down and felt Watusi's muscular arm grab me around the neck.

"Punk, we're gonna run you out of this neighborhood for sure," Watusi said, panting, as he shoved my face up against the wall.

"You might," I said, "but them white narcs with you ain't gonna touch me."

Something crashed into my back, just below the belt and I screamed in pain. One of the white bulls had hit me with his club.

"Hey man, take it easy," Watusi said, still breathing hard. I knew Watusi was hard, but I also knew he was fair. Unlike Babyface he wouldn't shoot a brother in the back, although he might mess his face up with his fists.

The narcs pulled me into a hallway, slammed my back up against the wall and began to search me. I was afraid. As long as I was out on the street I had a chance, but once the cops get you in a hall or alley they can do what they want.

"There it is, there it is," one of the narcs said.

I knew I was clean and looked at him in amazement. "Man, you jiving me. I don't have no dope on me."

"Well, there it is. It just fell out of your coat. Pick it up."

I looked at the floor and saw two glassine packs of heroin. "Hell man, I ain't picking up nothing that ain't mine. And that ain't mine."

Watusi interrupted. "That's enough, guys. I want him too, but I want him right."

"If he was clean then why did he run?" one of the white cops said.

Watusi walked over to me and reaching back, slapped me hard across the face. I felt my neck jerk as my head hit the wall. "Where'd you throw it, Youngblood?"

"Throw what, man? I don't know what you cats are talking about."

Watusi hit me again, this time in the stomach with his fist. I doubled over, my insides felt like they were going to come up my throat as I gagged for breath.

"Come on," Watusi said to the other cops. "He ain't gonna tell us nothing." They stepped out on the street and then Watusi stuck his head back in the hall. I had slumped to the floor, holding my stomach with both arms. "That was for your Aunt Rose," he said. "She don't deserve the likes of you. One day you're gonna break her heart, and when you do, then I'm gonna break your head. Just remember that."

I fell to one elbow and vomited on the floor.

Despite the constant hassles from the police, we were making big money, especially if we got a good sting. Then we were able to take off a good many days and spend the money until Barbara needed to go back to work.

One of my biggest problems was what to do with the cash. I couldn't have a bank account, because the secret of success in the game is to remain anonymous. It was the reason we never leased an apartment, but rented hotel suites where we could pay by the week without having to give credit references. The same was true with my car. I sold the first Caddy and got

an Eldorado. Only I didn't buy it myself. I gave
Bubby a few hundred extra and he agreed to have
the car in his name. If I ever got in any trouble with
it and they traced it, he would say it had been stolen.
I did invest some of our cash in what we called "re-
deemable merchandise," that is, things that could be
hocked if we needed quick cash—such as bailing Barbara out of jail. That's the reason I bought expensive
rings, watches, cuff links.

Most of my time was spent with Barbara. She was
constantly preening her body, realizing that unless
she kept it in perfect condition she would become
like all the other burned-out whores on the street. We
spent our afternoons in the steam baths. Sometimes
we would go to a movie or wind up in a swanky shop
buying dresses. Our early evenings were nearly always spent in the clubs or at a party in some apartment.

It was at one of these parties, in an apartment on
146th Street, that the game took on a new twist. This
street had a reputation. If a man was in trouble, this
is where he came. No white cop would dare come up
there, even in the daytime, and at night even the
black cops wouldn't walk there alone.

The party was thrown by some of the big-time
numbers boys. Barbara knew them all and when we
came in they gave us the hello. I wore a $250 suit with
velvet lapels, alligator shoes, and a $3000 diamond
ring; I could tell by Barbara's smile that she was
proud of me.

This wasn't just another gig. It was a party with a
lot of the big-timers present—the big names in
Harlem: jazz musicians, famous gamblers, hustlers. I
snorted a little coke and danced some with Barbara
and a few of the chicks when I noticed a beautiful
young girl sitting across the room staring at me. Her

jet-black hair was pulled back from her face re-
vealing high cheekbones, dark red lips and black-
berry eyes. I walked over and asked her if she wanted to dance. I didn't want to blow my good thing
with Barbara, but this was the most beautiful chick I
had ever seen. We danced. Then I got her a drink
and we sat at a table and talked. Her name was Toni.
She came from a rich family in the Bronx, had her
own car and a wad of bills. She had come to the
party with some dude who had gotten drunk and was
now shacked up in the bedroom.

Someone else stopped by the table and asked her
to dance. I walked back to the bar where Barbara
was sitting alone. She had been watching us.

"That's a nice girl," she said sipping her drink and
watching Toni as she moved expertly across the floor.
"You don't see many like that."

"You got something in mind?" I kidded her.

Barbara didn't like to be kidded about her Lesbian
tendencies. I watched the sullen expression move behind her eyes. But it was only there an instant and
then it was gone. "She could be a real money-maker
if things worked out," she said. "I bet you could pull
her if you'd try. We could double our take."

Mmm-hmmm," I agreed. "What should I do?"

"Let me talk to her," Barbara said. "I'll be back."
She got up, taking her drink with her.

A half hour later she was back. "She likes you. I
think she's ripe. Go to it."

There was no jealousy. It was all a business prop-
osition. Barbara knew what I was going to do and
where I would be doing it. It was all part of the
game.

I winked at Barbara and headed toward Toni. Moments later Toni got her wrap and we headed out.
We took her car, a white sports model with leopard

seats. We drove around the city talking. She was 19, had attended CCNY for a year. She was innocent, naive, tender.

We drove down into the Village and smoked some hash. I was leading her on, flashing big money and shooting her a line that she swallowed all the way up to the reel. In the early hours of the morning we got a hotel room together and I took her to bed. It was hard to believe, but she was a virgin.

The next morning she left me at the hotel and drove home to get a few clothes. She came back shortly after noon and we smoked some more hash together. I had never met a girl as hungry for love. When I gave her my line about how I had never loved anyone before, she bought the whole package. I stayed with Toni for a week. Twice during this time she took afternoons off and went home to pick up additional things. I used the time to go back to my apartment and bring Barbara up to date.

Toni knew absolutely nothing about me—where I got my money, what I did, where I lived. She was just caught up in the sensation of falling in love. Every night was launched with steaks and double scotches at a First Avenue bar in the Seventies. The other customers commented on my clothes, especially the new hat Barbara had bought me the week before, a Panama straw trimmed with peacock feathers.

"Men have always roughed you around, right?" I said to Toni. "You've always had to run from some guy who's not interested in anything but bedding you down. But not me. I want to touch you like velvet. You can cry to me, baby, and I'll kiss away the tears. ..." By the end of the week Toni's nose was open and I decided it was time to make my pitch.

"There's something I gotta tell you, baby," I said as

we got back to the hotel from a night at one of the clubs in Brooklyn. "I've got a problem."

She looked at me, nervously, her big black eyes searching my face. "What's wrong? You're not going to leave me, are you?" Her insecurity was so strong that she threw her arms around my neck and clung there. "I need you more than I've ever needed anyone in all my life. I don't care what kind of trouble you're in. I won't let you leave me!"

I lowered her down on the bed beside me and began to talk. She listened intently, her eyes searching my face for any evidence that I might be trying to back out of my relationship with her.

"I know I should have told you at the very beginning, but I was too much in love with you, and afraid if you knew you wouldn't want me."

"Oh no! You're all I want!"

"Several years ago when I was in the service I got strung out. I'm an addict."

"But that's no reason why you should leave me," she pleaded. "I don't care about that."

"I knew you'd be that way, baby," I said, kissing her. "But that's not all. I make my living as a pimp. That's the only way I can feed my habit."

"What do you mean?" she asked innocently. "I don't understand."

"Do you remember Barbara, the girl I was with at the party the night I met you?"

Toni nodded, never taking her eyes off my face.

"Well, Barbara works for me. We've got a place in Brooklyn and she hustles on the street for me. She's a prostitute."

I had read Toni right. She was an idealist. She loved me and would do anything to stay with me. "It doesn't   make   any   difference   what   you   are,

Youngblood. I love you. Can't you understand, I love you!"

"You've got to understand this, Toni. Barbara doesn't mean a thing to me: We just share the apartment together. But she's my living. And if you want to stay with me you'll have to move in with us."

A slight smile spread across her face as her eyes closed in relief. "I love you, darling. I love you."

The next afternoon Toni and I went to Brooklyn. Barbara moved into another room leaving Toni and me alone in the evenings while she was out on the street. Toni responded rapidly to this new way of life, seemingly content just to be with me. I realized it was time to begin to cut her loose.

Barbara had had a good night on Friday, and Saturday morning I took Toni to the city and bought her a new outfit. She'd had plenty of money as a kid, but never had had anyone take time to go out with her and buy her clothes. Her father owned a chain of restaurants and had always been too busy to spend time with his only daughter. I moved easily into that gap in her life, since time was the one commodity I had to give. It was all she really wanted.

That evening I took her out for a Saturday night in Harlem. After hitting some of the night spots I took her to a fancy restaurant and bar near the corner of 147th Street and St. Nicholas Avenue.

We came out about 1:30 a.m. and walked to the parking lot where we'd left my Eldorado. As I put the key in the car door, I heard a terrifying, high-pitched scream from the back seat of the car parked next to mine. Toni gasped and grabbed my arm.

"My God!" she said, "what was that?"

I knew what it was. It had come from my lips often

enough. It was the sound of a junkie without dope. I peered into the other car. It was an old Plymouth with dented fenders and the back window shattered out. On the back seat, curled into a fetal position, was a junkie, shaking, quivering, moaning. Toni shuddered. "What's wrong with him?"

"He's got a Jones, baby. He's strung out."

"Let's get out of here," she said. "I'm scared."

A sob came from the old car. I took one more look at the shivering junkie and opened my own car door. Toni scooted in, her face looking up at me in fright. I stared down at her, bit my lip in thought, and then turned back to the old Plymouth. Reaching into the inner pocket of my coat, I pulled out a tiny glassine envelope. Opening the door of the car I shook the huddled form on the seat. He looked up, his eyes staring from deep sockets in his head. "Here man," I said, poking the envelope at him. "Take it." He reached out a bony, quivering hand with broken nails. I dropped the package in his hand and slammed the door.

Climbing in beside Toni I twisted the key and the powerful engine of the Eldorado purred to life. "I must be getting soft," I said. "Giving away dope."

But the experience with the junkie proved to be the gambit I needed to move into another phase of the game designed to turn Toni out on the streets.

I waited a week and then on Friday night doubled over in a chair at the kitchen table as she came in from shopping.

"What's wrong, honey?" she screamed, dropping the groceries on the floor and rushing to me.

"I'm sick, baby, sick. I've got to have some dope."

"Where can I get it for you?" she said. "Tell me where to go."

"No baby, I don't have any money. It's all gone."

"But I thought that Barbara ..."

"No baby, you don't understand. We've spent it all. We don't have any money, at least not enough to get what I need."

Toni was scared. The experience with the addict in the parking lot was still vivid in her mind. "What can I do? I'll do anything. Just tell me."

"Barbara's not feeling well this week," I lied. "But you can go out there with her and she'll show you what to do. There's nothing to it."

"But I don't know what to do. I've never done anything like that. There must be some other way." She was almost frantic.

I faked some more stomach cramps, bending over and moaning. "If you really love me like you said you did you'd help me."

"Not that way, Youngblood, please not that way!"

I groaned again, dropping my head over between my knees. "Baby, Barbara and I never had the thing you and I have, yet she goes out all the time for me. I thought you loved me."

I played that card all the way, until finally she gasped, "I'll go, I'll go. I'll do anything for you, baby."

A half-hour later Toni and Barbara were in a cab together, heading downtown.

In the Belmont Plaza drugstore, Barbara told me later, she outfitted Toni with eye expanders—false lashes from Andrea's European Hair collection. Barbara chose Exotic Black. Then a gloss of Pearl Drops tooth polish and her pick of six varieties of hair dryers.

But out on the sidewalk again, Toni panicked, backing away from Barbara and finally fleeing into the street. Barbara caught up with her on Park Avenue. She reminded her that she had a man back in the apartment who believed in her, who was counting on her, who would suffer untold agony if she didn't produce for him.

And just then a fat pinky-ring John stepped out of the Belmont Plaza. "Just remember you're doing it for Youngblood," said Barbara. "Now go get him." And she pushed Toni out of the nest.

Barbara was right. Toni was going to be a good money-maker. She picked up $75 on her first trick, who turned out to be a rich dude from Denver town for a convention. She came back scared, but laughing. "He actually cried when I told him I was doing it for my boyfriend who was sick. He said he'd give me another $75 if I'd just spend the rest of the night with him and scratch his back."

It got in her blood. All night long peeking and hiding, zipping and lacing. Hustling the dollar, ducking the Third Division boys—young plainclothesmen assigned to the vice squad who work out of the 17th Precinct. The pace itself, the sheer velocity of risk, all were drugs.

Toni learned fast. Gucci shoes. Double Scotches. Kanekalon wigs. It was $10 tips to helpful bartenders, $15 to key doormen, and a $50 bill for the guard at a first-class hotel.

Within a month she was making four and five hundred a night. "That's a dollar a minute," she giggled one early morning when I picked the two of them up in my Eldorado.

Barbara nodded her head. "We're on our way, man."

12

DEATH TRIP

What can I, a poor black woman, do to destroy America? This is a question, with appropriate variations, being asked in every black heart. There is one answer—I can kill. There is one compromise—I can protect those who kill. There is one cop-out—I can encourage others to kill. There are no other ways.

—Nikki Giovanni

I HAD been in a club in Harlem on 145th Street, had gotten high and was drinking beer with a couple of cats.

"You hear about Cadillac Walter?" one of them said.

"He's moved up to the big time," said the other. "He's running stuff for the organization."

I knew what the organization was. The Mafia. I also knew something about a dope runner. He was the guy who picked the stuff up from the boat or wherever it came in, cut it, and then handed it out to the street pushers. There was big money in it, but best of all you had enough dope, always, to feed your own habit.

"How do you get into a thing like that?" I asked.

The cats glanced at each other and then back at

me. "You don't. They come to you. And man, don't go
around asking a lot of questions either. Dudes who do
that don't come down to breakfast some morning."

I finished my beer and went outside. The street
that night was filled with funky girls. The panic was
over, but dope was still hard to find. I had connections in Brooklyn, but the prostitutes who were
strung out were really up tight. I could tell if a girl
was a junkie by the way she looked: her skin would
be faded. Even if she wasn't high, she would look
dingy.

I walked up to 146th Street looking at the chicks.
"Say baby, you sporting tonight?" I heard a voice behind me.

Without even turning around I answered casually,
"Sure, mama, if I could find the right sport to do it
with."

The voice dropped to a whisper. "How you doing,
Aaron?" Very, very few people called me Aaron. I
jerked my head around and there she stood, a memory from the dirty living room floor of Bobby's
shabby apartment in Brooklyn. "Coreen! What are
you doing here?"

She looked up at me. "Now ain't that a silly question?"

I thought about it, and it was. But how different
she looked from those kid days when we had jugged
on her floor. Already she looked withered, like the old
crones in Grand Central. I knew what she was doing
out there. She was trying to raise enough money to
feed her habit.

"Come on, girl, get off this corner. What the hell is
wrong with you? Come on over here and let me buy
you some coffee and send you back home."

She let me buy her the coffee. "Now look, I've got
to make some money," she said.

"I'll give you the money."

"Okay. Thanks. But tomorrow night it's going to be the same thing."

I knew what she was talking about, but I gave her the money anyhow. It was kind of for Bobby.

This experience with Coreen showed me the importance of having your prostitutes hooked on heroin so they would have to work for a living, game or no game. I knew I could never get Barbara hooked, she was too clever. But Toni . . .

I talked it over with Barbara one night and she agreed. The following afternoon, we were all in the apartment. We had slept late, fixed a 3 p.m. breakfast and were lounging around smoking some hashish. I went into the bedroom, got my needle, and started preparing a fix.

Suddenly Barbara turned to Toni. "Have you ever had a fix?"

Toni was startled. "No. Why?"

"Oh, I don't know. I was just watching you while he was cooking up and you seemed interested."

"Have you ever had any?" Toni asked.

"Sure," Barbara answered, "but it didn't turn me on. I liked it to begin with but it grew old. I'd rather stick to coke."

"What's it like?" Toni said, her interest building.

"Great, baby," I grinned as I pulled the liquid into the needle. "Fix her up," I said to Barbara, "and I'll let her try one out."

"I don't know," Toni said, hesitating. "Will I become addicted?"

"Not with one shot, or even a dozen," Barbara said as she pulled up Toni's sleeve. "He'll just give you a skin pop and you can tell if you like it or not."

She liked it. The next day I gave her another one. She liked it even more. Two nights later she took one herself and within two weeks, with me supplying all the dope she could use, she was hooked. I gave her her first mainline shot myself.

Then Barbara took over again, working Toni on one corner while she worked another. From then on it was no game with Toni, because dope is always for real.

I found out just how real it still was in my own life a month later when I was suddenly faced with the prospect of kicking cold turkey again.

I was sitting in my apartment alone, watching television. I had done something I seldom did, let Barbara and Toni take my car. They had been gone for about an hour when the phone rang. It was Toni.

"I'm in trouble," she said.

Toni was calling from a pay phone on a corner near Central Park. She and Barbara had been arrested by a couple of white cops. Ordinarily I would have let them go on to jail and bailed them out the next day, but this time they had the car, and the car was dirty—I knew there was a bundle under the back seat. But the cops didn't want the bust. They wanted some money. That's why they let Toni make the call.

I caught a cab and got out around the corner from where the cop car was sitting behind my Eldorado. I showed up clean. No gun. No dope. No identification because I suspected a trap, like they were using the girls as a decoy. I walked up to where the girls were sitting in the car. The cops were sitting in their car behind, the motor running and the windows closed.

"Hey, baby, what's happening?" I said nonchalantly. "Haven't seen you two in a long time."

I stood there rapping with the girls and the two cops stayed in the car behind. Barbara was at the wheel and said, "I think they want to make a deal. It's time for them to go home, you know."

I walked back to the police car and the driver rolled down his window. "What happened, officer? Can I help?"

We were all playing the game and I realized whoever played it best won. The officer at the wheel said, "Well, this girl is in some mighty big trouble. We stopped them for going through a stop light and found the heroin in her purse."

"Ah, I see. I didn't know you could search someone without a warrant." I didn't want to make them mad so I kept my voice friendly.

"We didn't have to search her," the cop answered. "She opened her purse to get her driver's license and this heroin fell out in the street."

"Oh ... I see ... Wow, officer. That's too bad. I mean, these are real nice chicks. Clean. You know. What can be done? I know you don't want to flag them, you know, give them a break."

"Now it was their move. I waited to see how they would come on. "Well, it's getting late," the other cop said, "and we're going off. We really don't want to make an arrest. They seem like nice girls."

We were still playing the game. I knew better than to ask "What will it cost me?" so I finally put the question to them, "Well ... ah ... I got three hundred. Think that will handle it?"

The pig at the wheel looked at the other cop, then looked back. "Okay, get in the back seat and I'll tell the girls they can go on."

Relieved I crawled into the back of the patrol car and slipped the cash out of my pocket while the cop who was behind the wheel got out and told Barbara she could go. I waited until the car had turned the corner and the officer had returned before slipping the cash through the steel grate that separated the seats. The two cops counted it and then the one next of the driver turned around and said, "I think there's been some kind of misunderstanding. You said three hundred apiece."

"Screw it man," I said. "You got wax in your ears." I grabbed the door handle to get out only to realize that I was locked in. The only way the door could be opened was from the ouside. I was trapped.

"Man, that's all I got. Don't hassle me over something I ain't got. I just wanted to do those girls a favor, that's all."

"Three hundred each or we take you to jail," the cop said grimly. "We got to check in at the station before we leave and we might as well take you along."

Something snapped inside me. I had played the game by the rules but they hadn't. I began to curse and scream. The cop just shrugged his shoulders. "Let's go. Looks like we've got a disorderly conduct in the back."

At the precinct they opened the back door and I came out swinging. It was just what they wanted; one of them hit me on the back of the head and then stepped back and let me fall face first to the pavement. My head was swimming and I felt blood pouring down the front of my suit. "Looks like we'll have to add a resisting arrest to the charge," one of them said, as he yanked me to my feet and shoved me into the station. I knew I would be out the next day, but I also knew it had been three hours since I had had a fix and by morning I would be in pain, real pain.

It was noon the next day before Barbara paid me out. By then I was doubled over in cramps. She was driving my car and took me straight to a shooting gallery on 114th Street where I got a set of works and fixed. In seconds the pain had eased and I was okay again. I walked slowly back out to the car and Barbara drove me back home. But I was in sorry shape. Every bone and nerve in my body ached from the hours I had spent going through withdrawal. The back of my head had a lump the size of a lemon and the blood was caked on my face and shirt. I knew I was going to have to go through another methadone program or die, my habit was too strong.

This time I admitted myself to Manhattan General. I remained in the hospital thirty days until the heroin habit, for the first time in all my years of addiction, was completely squelched. Of course, I was now hooked on methadone, but I had gained weight and was giving serious consideration to just staying on methadone, tapering off little by little, until I was clean.

Almost every night in the hospital, too, I dreamed of Aunt Rose. It had been almost a year since I had seen her and I felt a sudden yearning to go home.

"She ain't here," the building superintendent said when I couldn't get in the apartment.

"When will she be back?"

"She ain't coming back."

I felt a wave of panic washing over me. Even though I had only seen her a few times since coming home from Korea, she was the person who was always there. This was home. If I needed a place to sleep I could come here. If I was sick, I could come here. My throat felt dry, like dust.

"Where'd she go?"

"I don't know. She left about three weeks ago. Sold her beauty shops too."

I wanted to sit down, but leaned against the wall

instead. He continued. "She left a note for you. Wait here and I'll go get it."

I sat on the front steps of the apartment, where I had sat as a little boy, and read Aunt Rose's letter. She said she and Uncle Arthur couldn't stay here any longer; someone had found out about the house in Bergen Street and how I was making my money and by now it was all over the neighborhood. They had lived in this apartment for 20 years. She had worked in Brooklyn most of her life. She was giving it all up, her business, her friends, her home. She left no forwarding address.

Slowly, deliberately, I tore the letter in two. Then folding it I tore it again and again as I sat staring blankly at the building across the street. The gray stone church stared back, silent, cold. I stacked the torn scraps of paper neatly on the bottom step and watched as the wind whipped the top pieces off the stack and sent them bouncing and scampering down the dirty sidewalk.

Gradually the stack grew smaller until all the pieces were gone. It had been a long time since I'd felt like crying, but I felt it welling up inside me as it had within the little boy who sat in the dark behind the bathtub. This time I didn't cry. Instead I walked to where I had parked my car, drove back across the Brooklyn Bridge, went straight to the apartment and took a fix. It was the first one in 30 days but it was as though I had never been off.

While I had been in the hospital Barbara and Toni had moved into a new area of prostitution. Both were now working as call girls, their base of action being the big midtown hotels near Times Square. The money was bigger, the hours better, the work easier and the danger of getting beaten up or robbed much less.

With money pouring in my habit once again soared, this time up to $80 a day. We changed hotels three times, moving each time into a swankier suite. There seemed to be no limit to the source of money and our only problem was where to spend it.

"Whitey!" The name was on the lips of every black in Harlem. "Kill Whitey!" No one was willing to go South to help out, but the hate that came over TV and through the newspapers was enough to fire us to violence.

That summer the ghetto smarted as news reached us of Martin Luther King's march from Selma to Montgomery. Bull Connor's dogs didn't just bite Alabama blacks, they bit the soul of every black in America. Dick Gregory returned from Alabama and spoke in the clubs and churches of Harlem. "Good evening, ladies and gentlemen. I know the South very well. I spent twenty years there one night . . ." We laughed at Gregory but the malice of Southern prejudice was matched only by the hate generated in the steam of Harlem's ghetto.

Occasionally I would see Rat on the streets that summer. He had been in Sing Sing and had come out a Black Muslim. One night I spotted him lounging outside of a small bar on Seventh Avenue and 146th. He told me that Charlie and Dozie of the Mice were doing one to five in the federal prison at Danbury, Connecticut, and that Dozie had become a Black Muslim too. I'd seen these Muslims; they were always preaching down at the corner of Seventh and 125th. I had walked by one time and seen the people standing around listening to Malcolm X. He was preaching about Muhammad and the people were all clapping their hands saying, "Yes, Yes."

Rat began to tell me more about the Muslims. "They're into things, man. A new day has dawned and Malcolm is gonna set us free."

"Free from what, man?"

"From the white devils who've stole from us and poisoned our minds."

I looked at him. "You all right, Rat?"

"Yeah man, I know you ain't heard much of this but I been to Sing Sing and all the cats in Sing Sing are Muslims. Do you know that you are a black god?"

"Oh man. What kind of junk you been taking?" I laughed.

"No man, believe me. The white man was made by a black scientist, in a test tube, man. Whitey ain't even real. He's like a robot, a monster."

"Where'd you get that stuff?" I said.

"From the Muslims, man, that's what I been telling you."

"And you believe it, Rat?"

"Don't call me Rat no more. I got a new name. It's Bashar."

"What you mean you got a new name?"

"That's right. Your real name ain't johnson. That's just some name a slave owner hung on your grand-paw because his pappy was a white plantation owner named John. Your name ain't John-son, it's *Abdullah*."

"Man, you're off your rocker."

"No man, this Muslim bit is where it's at. We're black men, and yet we're ashamed of our blackness. Your aunt used to sell makeup, didn't she? What was her best product? I bet it was something to take black hair and make it look like Whitey's hair. Malcolm says he used to conk his hair with lye until it burned his scalp off, trying to look like a white man. Now he's been set free and can be black. Black is beautiful, man, black is beautiful."

There were a lot of changes in Rat. Because of this new religion of his he didn't drink anymore. He didn't eat pork. But the amazing thing to me was that he didn't stutter anymore.

"Maybe you got something, uh ... Bashar?"

"Something else, brother," Bashar said, looking me straight in the face. "These black preachers going around preaching about the white god ... they're just playing a game."

"Man, all hustlers know that," I grinned.

"They saw it right from the beginning, right after slavery," Bashar continued. "When a cat started preaching, that meant he didn't have to work no more. He got the callin'. It was an easy life. Instead of kneeling down in the cotton patch weeding the cotton, he was kneeling in front of some sister. It's all a game, man. There's only one God and his name is Allah."

Bashar was steaming as he talked. "The black man is lost, and Muhammad is trying to show him the way. Look at me, man. Remember how I was strung out? Now I'm clean and I ain't never going back to the old life. Muhammad has given us something to fight for, man."

Bashar stepped back and I saw he was about to get personal. "You junkies have to use drugs, man, to stand this life. Nobody can stand it without something. I was on em too, but not anymore. Man, I'm a prince. I'm too powerful to be made a slave ever again. My mind is free. Nobody can enslave you when your mind is free."

Bashar put his hand on my shoulder, looking deep into my face. "Tell Whitey to look out 'cause Black Power's gonna get his mama. Remember, Allah is black. Salaam, aleikum, brother." He turned and walked down the street.

13

BIG TIME

> *Look at him laugh. He's really not laughing,*
> *he's just laughing with his teeth ... The white*
> *man doesn't know how to laugh. He just shows*
> *his teeth. But WE know how to laugh. We*
> *laugh deep down, from the bottom up.*
>
> —Malcolm **X**

ONE BLUSTERY cold February night Toni, Barbara and I went to a party in Harlem. The usual people were there, the runners, the pimps, the gamblers, the prostitutes. I had become pretty well known in most of the places—those places that were frequented by the money-makers—in Harlem, as well as the busier, active spots in Brooklyn. When I came in people would turn and look. "Hey, Youngblood, you must be making some money." I played the game back and somewhere in between the lies we all knew where each other stood. Some of the prostitutes wanted me to be their man but I wouldn't take them on. Toni and Barbara were enough and I didn't want these small-time whores in with them, getting busted and me having to bail them out all the time.

At the party in Harlem everyone was snorting coke and smoking hashish when I was approached by a short stocky little guy. "Say, some of my people have been trying to get in contact with you. They been asking about you."

"What people is this?" I asked, reaching for a drink on the bar and flicking a tiny particle off my new velvet jacket.

"I have some friends that I think you would be interested in, friends who are interested in you." He handed me a match book with a number written on the inside. "Call this number. I think you'll be pleased."

But I had too much going to call the number.

Three weeks later I had gone to the Uptown Gym on 125th Street to watch some of the fighters work out. The gym was right next to the Apollo Theatre, and coming out of the gym I bumped into someone going into the Apollo. As I turned around, I saw it was this same stocky little fellow.

"How's it going, Youngblood?" he said.

"Okay, man."

"My friends are still interested in hearing from you."

"Man. I think I lost that number you gave me," I said.

"I wouldn't keep them waiting too long if I were you. You might be missing a good thing."

The man gave me another match cover with a number. That night I talked to Barbara about it.

"I don't like it," she said. "There's been some dudes around here too, asking questions about you. I never seen them before."

"I don't think this cat's a cop, though," I said. "Sounds like something else."

"Why don't you call the number and find out," Toni said.

I shrugged my shoulders and reached for the

phone. A deep voice answered. "This is Youngblood," I said, and waited.

"We've been wanting to talk to you."

"Who's we, man?"

"Don't get up tight," the voice said. "We'd just like to talk to you."

"Man, the last time I talked to someone I wound up in jail."

"That must have been the time you tried to bribe those cops down near Central Park."

I gulped. "Hey man, how'd you know?"

There was a moment's silence. Then the voice closed the conversation by saying if I ever wanted to talk, call again and ask for Gino.

I hung up and reported to Barbara. "It smells like the syndicate to me," she said. "Play it slow, baby, play it slow."

Three weeks later I called the number again. This time the voice on the other end told me to call another number. I did. "Let me talk to Gino," I said.

"Yeah? Who's this?"

"Youngblood."

"What number you calling from?"

I told him I was at a pay phone in the back of a bar in Brooklyn. "Wait beside the phone," the voice said. "You'll get a call inside five minutes."

Three minutes later the phone rang. I recognized the deep voice from before. "I'd like to meet you and talk. Dinner some night this week?"

I was caught off guard. "Well, ah, sure, whatever you say."

"Fine," he said warmly. "What about Patsy's tomorrow at seven?"

"Uh, sure," I said, not expecting him to pick such a public place.

I was in front of Patsy's at 6:45. Promptly at 7:00 a

car glided to a stop in front of the door. A man stepped out and the car slipped back into the traffic on 56th. The man turned and greeted me.

"Youngblood!" I knew better than to talk. I adhered to the prime rule of the hustler, ask no questions, give no answers.

"Gino" was in his early forties, very Westchester. He put his arm on my shoulder and steered me into the restaurant.

Barbara was right; this was the syndicate. But what did the syndicate want with me? This man must be small-potatoes in the organization to fool with a nobody like me. He made me wonder what the real power must be like.

"Uh, what's this all about?" I asked.

He shook his head, picking up the wine list. "We have all evening. Let's not spoil our time at the table with talk of business. Life is too short not to enjoy the good things."

I knew he was grandstanding but I enjoyed it. He ordered for us. When the wine came he smelled the cork, tasted the sample, shook his head and spoke rapidly in Italian. The waiter retrieved the bottle and left, returning in moments with another. This time the waiter was allowed to fill our glasses. My host toasted the "future" and we sat and talked.

When the salad arrived he shook his head again and motioned to the ever-hovering waiter, who snatched it away. Moments later the waiter was back with fresh bowls of salad and my host smiled his approval. I thought I was a master at running games, but this guy was the real thing.

After dinner we talked. "I'm glad you're doing all right, Youngblood," he said. "My friends and I, we like people who use their heads. Most guys, the only way they get ahead is busting someone else's. Me, I don't even own a gun. I bet you don't have one either."

"Of course not," I lied. "If I can't think my way out of a tight spot I might as well become a street junkie."

He chuckled. "Excellent. Now I want you to think about something else."

I was listening to his language. Not once did he say a thing that could ever be used against him. He was a cool, cool cat. Yet the more he talked the more I realized he knew all about me. He knew who I was buying dope from. He knew about the girls.

"How would you like to work for us?" he said abruptly.

I stayed in the game. "Doing what? I'm not hungry. I keep my habit together."

"My friends and I need a young black like you to work with blacks. We want you to pick up a package for us from time to time and maybe make some deliveries. With whatever help you need, of course."

I knew what he was talking about. He never used the term heroin, runner or pusher. But I knew, and he knew I knew.

"Think about it and let me know." He snapped his fingers and the bill appeared. He paid for it by dropping a fifty on the tray and waving the waiter away.

The moment we reached the curb his limousine pulled up from its parking place in the tow-away zone down the street. As we shook hands, he glanced at my shoes and said, "I must get a pair like those," and he was gone.

"Man," said Barbara after I told her about the evening, "that's the big time. What you going to do?"

"I thought maybe you might know him," I said.

"Not him, baby," she said. "I wish I did. But cats like that never mess around the street. I bet he belongs to a church, goes to PTA meetings and takes his wife and kids on picnics."

"You reckon this dude is one of the family?"

"Not him! He's just a peon, man. He's the errand boy they send to talk to guys. You never will see any of the family. Nobody does."

The next day I called the number my host had given me. The voice on the other end of the wire said, "Expect a call at 3 p.m. tomorrow."

My caller the next day told me to hire 12 men. He never told me what for but I knew. I was to become a heroin runner.

I spent the next two days on the street rounding up dudes to work as my pushers. About half of them came from Brooklyn, the rest from Harlem. All were junkies, all jumped at the job.

"You gonna need a strong-arm guy," Barbara said one afternoon as we were riding the subway from Brooklyn back to our current hotel in the city. "You're going to need protection."

I knew just the man. Charlie was fresh out of prison and Charlie knew how to cut heroin. I put out the word in a couple of bars that I was looking for him and the next afternoon he was waiting in front of my apartment.

Charlie had turned 30, his Afro was longer, and his weight had fallen off—due to his heavy coke consumption.

"I got me a backer," I said swinging down the street as we fell into step, "and I need someone with a piece to stand beside me."

Charlie examined his knuckles, cracking them one by one as we walked along the sidewalk. "What you dealing?" he asked.

"What else is there in this town?" I said without saying. "I got me a dozen cats working for me and I don't trust any of them. I need somebody I can trust and—ah, somebody who knows how to cut stuff."

"Sounds like you're moving up, baby. What you want me to do?"

"Just stay close, man. Check with me tomorrow about six and see what's cooking."

The next afternoon, Friday, I received another call. "Pick up a package at four this afternoon. It'll be in a shopping bag in the coffee shop of the Long Island Railroad station on Flatbush Extension and Atlantic in Brooklyn." There was a sharp click and the phone went dead. I had my first order.

It was hard to imagine a quarter kilo of uncut heroin worth more than $100,000 left unattended in a coffee shop. Yet I was soon to learn that packages left in public places were much safer than packages hidden away. All of my pickups from that time on, with the exception of the one which nearly cost me my life, would be made in public places.

That afternoon I took the subway to Atlantic and Flatbush and made for the coffee shop. Everywhere I saw suspicious looking people. Two men were loitering near the phone booths in the middle of the lobby; they glanced at me as I passed. Cops or Mafia lookouts? A couple of uniformed cops stood just outside the door to the café, smoking cigarettes and munching on candy bars. One of them stared hard at me as I approached, but I ignored him and walked into the restaurant.

I took a seat at the counter and ordered a cup of coffee. There were four other people in the café. Two black teen-age girls were sitting at a table reading comic books. An old man sat alone, eating, and at the next table was a tired looking man in a faded gray coat, drinking coffee and reading a newspaper. Beside him, in a chair pulled up close against the table, was a paper shopping bag. I felt my heart quicken.

I sipped my coffee, looking at his back, waiting for him to leave. Finally he rose, folded his paper, and walked away from the table. He left the shopping bag in the chair. I planned to let him get out of the room before going after the bag. He passed me, never giving a sign of recognition, paid his bill and left the restaurant.

I was reaching into my pocket for a coin to pay for my coffee when I felt someone sit down beside me, between me and the table where the bag was. Startled I looked up. All I could see was blue. It was a cop. Watusi.

"Been a long time, Johnson," he said, motioning to the waitress behind the counter to bring him coffee.

I tried to keep the panic out of my voice. "Listen man, I'm clean," I said. "I been up to Manhattan General. I took the cure."

"Sure, sure," Watusi said, sipping his coffee and looking straight ahead. I looked beyond him at the table where the bag was, and then out the door into the subway station. The man in the gray coat was talking to a dark-skinned man with a wool cap. Graycoat walked away and woolcap walked over and stood in the door, watching me.

"Understand your Aunt Rose couldn't take no more."

The palms of my hands were covered with sweat. "No man, you got it all wrong. She got a good offer and moved to Buffalo. I hear from her all the time. In fact, I was up to see her last week."

Watusi set the coffee cup down and turned and looked at me. Over his shoulder I could see woolcap, his piercing eyes never leaving me. *He thinks I'm selling out.*

"That was a good woman," Watusi said, "and you broke her heart."

"No man, that's not so. I love my Aunt Rose. That's the reason I took the cure. I won't ever touch the stuff again. I've gone straight."

An old woman had come in the door. She was dressed in a long, faded brown coat and her stockings were twisted on her legs. She was heading toward the table where the bag was.

"The only place you're going straight is straight to hell," Watusi said.

The old woman was sitting down at the table. She was putting her pocketbook in the chair with the bag. The man at the door took a short step inside.

"When will you junkies ever learn?" Watusi said. "Addicts are dying like flies on my beat. Little girls are out tricking. What we need is a good fire in Brooklyn like they had in Chicago. It kills the vermin."

She saw it. She saw the bag. She was getting up and taking it out of the chair.

"The junkies have gone wild. They're snatching pocketbooks in broad daylight, beating up old ladies."

She was looking in the bag. She was picking up the box in the bottom of the bag. I could see it. It was the size of a cigar box and wrapped in gift paper tied with a ribbon.

"Last week some of your junkie friends robbed a truck on my beat."

She was turning to the man at the next table, trying to give him the bag. He was shaking his head.

"Guess what was in it? Toilet Paper! A truckload of toilet paper!"

She was taking the bag to the two young girls at the other table. One of them was holding the box, shaking it, laughing.

"These junkies stripped that truck clean. Stole every case of toilet paper."

Now the old woman was heading this way. She was bringing the bag to Watusi.

"Just remember, Johnson, stay off my beat if you want to stay healthy." Watusi rose, flipped a dime on the counter and walked toward the door.

I glanced at the old woman. She put one hand halfway up as if to flag him. But he was already out the door, brushing past the man in the wool cap. The old woman turned around and went back to her table. She put the bag on the chair and sat down to eat her sandwich. I sat and waited, my blood pounding.

Ten minutes later she got up to go, leaving the bag on the chair. As she started toward the cash register I passed her in the opposite direction, picked up the bag and headed for the outside door. I supposed she would report the bag to the clerk at the register but it would be too late. I was long gone.

That night, Barbara, Toni, Charlie and I took a cab down into the Village where we got a hotel room. In fact, we got two rooms. But we only used one—to cut the heroin in.

Charlie took the full-length mirror off the bathroom door and laid it on the floor after wiping it clean with a towel. Then I untied the wrappings on the package. Inside was a cigar box, and inside the cigar box was a clear plastic bag filled with fine white powder. It was more heroin than I had ever seen in all my life.

"Man, look at all that horse," Toni said, her eyes wide. "Look at all that horse."

"Let's get with it," I said. I gently emptied the contents of the bag on the mirror. Charlie took out clothes hangers and bent them straight. Then he and Barbara used them to spread the raw, uncut heroin out over the surface of the mirror.

Charlie had come prepared. He reached in a sack and brought out the four other necessary ingredients: powdered milk, powdered sugar, white bonita and quinine.

"Always add the quinine last," Charlie warned, as he sprinkled the powdered milk and sugar into the heroin. "If you don't it'll eat up the heroin."

Next he added the bonita for "body" and finally the bitter quinine. We used the coat hangers to mix it, taking care that not a speck fell off the mirror. Then, using the straight edge of a piece of cardboard, we piled it in the center of the mirror and, lifting it on the cardboard, put it in one of Toni's nylon stockings. Holding the stocking over the mirror we shook it gently so the powder sifted back onto the mirror. This not only strained out the few seeds still in the heroin, but thoroughly mixed it for packaging. It didn't take us long to realize that by holding our heads close we could get high on the dust.

Next came the tedious process of bagging the dope. From a contact in Harlem Charlie had bought a whole suitcase full of small glassine bags, the kind used by stamp collectors. These were the "nickel" bags which would sell on the street for $5 apiece. Each pusher would get a share of them and in turn would keep ten percent of his take. I was supposed to get ten percent of the overall take, the rest went back to the banker.

It was almost dawn before we got the last of the dope bagged and taped. We bagged some as spoons which sold for $20, some in $10 capsules. The final thing I did was divide it evenly into 12 parts, keeping out enough to last Toni, Charlie and me for the rest of the week. It had been a long night's work, but I was in business. I was a runner.

14

HELL'S IRON GATE

> *Young man—*
> *Young man—*
> *Your arm's too short to box with God.*
> *Young man—*
> *Young man—*
> *Smooth and easy is the road*
> *That leads to hell and destruction.*
> *Down grade all the way,*
> *The further you travel, the faster you*
> * go.*
> *No need to trudge and sweat and toil,*
> *Just slip and slide and slip and slide*
> *Till you bang up against hell's iron*
> * gate.*
>
> —James Weldon Johnson

I MADE my way up the narrow, creaky stairs of a tenement off Warren in Brooklyn. My telephone contact said the stuff would be in the closet in an abandoned apartment on the fourth floor. I had been making pickups for more than six months now, about one a week, but this was the first one in a hidden place. It bothered me.

Light filtered through a broken windowpane on the landing of the stairs as I felt my way through the stinking debris. In one apartment I could hear sounds

150

of activity, a flushing toilet and the accompanying gurgle of water down the pipes through the walls, muffled shouts of men and women arguing. I brushed a cobweb from my face and grimaced at the stench of vomit and piss. Even though the tenement had been abandoned, it was still used by junkies for a toilet or a place to escape the cold.

I finally reached the fourth floor and made my way to the front right apartment where the stuff was supposed to be hidden. The rotting floor shivered with each step and as I approached the door I heard the sound of scurrying rats along the floor and in the walls. The door was ajar. I started to push it open when I heard voices. At first I thought they were coming from the stairwell but then I realized they were coming from inside the room.

I gently pushed the door and saw two young blacks sitting on the floor. Between them was my pack of heroin. They were high. They had opened the stuff and shot it right there—raw.

"You sure them other guys coming?" one of them said.

"Yeah man, I told em what we got."

It was time for me to leave, quick. Down the steps and just as I stepped through the door I saw a gang of young kids, maybe a dozen of them between the ages of 13 and 15, rounding the corner. They saw me coming out the front door of the building and stopped. I kept walking across the street to where my car was parked. In the rear-view mirror I saw them dash on into the tenement. It would be a night of great celebration for them, but in the morning the papers would report two 13-year-old kids had been found in a condemned apartment, dead from an overdose.

The syndicate held me responsible for the loss.

"You stung us on that delivery," the anonymous voice on the other end of the telephone said.

"Man, I didn't sting you. I was there on time, and I was in the right place. Those kids had already gotten the package and were calling their friends. If anyone's to blame it's the cat who decided to leave the stuff up there to begin with. Man, don't ever leave stuff in a place like that. Put it out in the open. No one will mess with it there."

The voice grunted. But from then on we used public places only. Sometimes I would make the pickup from a phone booth near the docks in Brooklyn. The package would be left under the seat or on top of the phone itself. Other times I would be directed to Grand Central or Penn Station, or one of the subway stations. Sometimes the telephone instructions would describe a man. I would go in the washroom and the guy would hand me a newspaper. Inside would be a locker key. Other times he would whisper as we passed, "The end phone booth." I would go to the booth and find a locker key in the return coin slot.

I could see now why the syndicate wanted me and my friends. They had to recruit a lot of people. I seldom saw the drop-off man and when I did he was always a different stranger.

It was all a game. If the evidence wasn't actually in the man's possession, he couldn't be arrested. Hollowed-out shoe heels, fake hat-linings, these things were old stuff to the narcs. I devised my own way to keep from getting caught with the stuff on me. I would carry the bundle inside my coat wrapped in a newspaper, holding it against my body with my arm. If anybody looked like fuzz I'd go through a door, or turn a corner or duck into an alley, loosening my arm enough to let the package drop. If I decided I had been mistaken I'd go back and get my stuff. However, there were several junkies in the city who never knew who it was that had left a gift for them on the street.

Money was exchanged the same way. I would take the money as it came in, put it in a shoebox, and leave it in a trash can, a phone booth, a laundromat, a parked car. Again, I rarely saw the pickup man. To my knowledge I never lost a money delivery, although one time a shoebox holding $100,000 almost got away.

It was late afternoon and I had been instructed to leave the box on a bench in Central Park. I bought a hot dog from one of the vendors and sat eating. When I finished, I casually dropped my newspaper on top of the shoebox and walked away. At the end of the path I turned around and saw a young couple who had appeared out of nowhere examing the box. I knew better than to return, so I just loitered near an iron trash can, waiting to see what was going to happen.

Wrapping the box in the newspaper, they started away. As they rounded the corner I noticed two men following them. It was one of the few times that I had ever seen any of the pickup men. I kept moving. The next day the papers carried a story about a senseless killing in Central Park.

Money was flowing in in quantities so great it was impossible to count. Sometimes our take for the week was so much that we just stuffed it in a clothes hamper in whatever hotel apartment we were occupying. Meanwhile my habit had soared back up to $110 a day, but as long as the junk was available it didn't matter.

Everybody in the game expected to O.D. or be busted sooner or later. It was just a matter of hanging on as long as you could. It was a funny thing about O.D.s. Barbara had a theory that a good O.D.

was what every junkie was really after. One night after we had been down to my favorite spot for a few drinks Barbara started telling me about her former pimp, a junkie named Fred. "It's like he was always after an O.D., like it was the ultimate high," she said as we cruised south on Fifth Avenue. "If he heard some junkie had croaked from an O.D. right away he'd start talking, 'Hey, did you hear that so-and-so O.D.'d in the Bronx? Wonder where he got his stuff?' He figured if the cat O.D.'d it was because he had picked up some super-dope someplace and he'd be off trying to find where he could get some of the same stuff."

"Aw, baby, nobody really wants to knock off," I argued.

Barbara stuck to her point. "Don't be so sure, baby. There's two kinds of junkies who do crazy things, them that can't get dope when they need it, and them that has too much all the time. Fred was the one with too much and he was always looking for that bigger high. Like you give a cat some superfantastic dope and he shoots up and is dreaming and so high he can't even pick up his head. And you say to him, 'Ain't that fantastic dope?' And the cat says, 'Yeah, but it could have been better. . . .' See what I mean? He's right on the edge, on the high of his life, barely alive, and he is saying it could have been better. Better means O.D., baby. O.D. That's what all the cats really want."

I drove in silence. Barb didn't know what she was talking about. She didn't take junk so how could she know. It was stupid to think that one day I would grow tired of clothes and money and highs and crawl into a stinking back room of a shooting gallery and end it all with a deliberate O.D. Stupid.

In fact, my biggest problem right now was where to keep the money. Five thousand wrinkled bills take up a lot of space. Once a week we would sort it out and wrap it in rubber bands so it could be squeezed into a box for delivery.

Since we had to remain anonymous, we also had to be on the move, always living in hotels, of course. We spent as much as we could. My last Cadillac was painted gold with leopard-skin seat covers. I got a friend of mine who owned a barbershop to buy it for me—cash. Since I had lent him ten grand to start him in business, he was obligated. Later we set up a gambling parlor in the back of the barbershop. It gave me a good place to hang out and to spend some money too.

One Saturday night we were back there playing poker. Some of the boys were making a lot of noise and the police had come in, but my friend gave them twenty apiece and they left without ever checking the back. About midnight, though, three big black cats came in. I was looking at my poker hand and we had almost $10,000 on the table when I heard a voice behind me. "Don't a nigger move."

I had heard that tone of voice only once before, and that was when we got held up in a crap game in Tommy Turk's basement on 145th Street. I turned my head, slowly, and saw two cats standing just inside the door that led from the barbershop. Both of them had shotguns. Behind them, with his back to them and facing the barbershop was another cat with a shotgun.

Charlie was across the table from me and started to get up, but one of the cats pointed his barrel at him and said, "Freeze, nigger. Don't even breathe." Charlie stopped statue-still, in that half-up, half-down position.

"Backs against the wall," the other man said. We all rose and slowly backed up against the wall, hands high over our heads. One of the cats put his double-barreled gun right up against my face. I could smell gunpowder and knew the gun had to have been fired recently.

All I could see were those two black ominous holes. They were the biggest holes I had ever looked into. I thought again of Tommy Turk's basement and how Tommy gave one of the gunmen some lip. That dude didn't even blink an eye, he just pulled the trigger and Tommy's head splattered all over the wall. It wasn't dying I thought about, it was my brains and bones splashed around.

"Don't breathe." The man reached out and stripped a ring off my finger. It was a $3000 diamond but I didn't even think about it. All I thought about was not breathing and listening as close as I could to see if the man was telling me to do something, so I could cooperate. The other man was scraping the cash off the table and putting it in a paper sack.

The cats backed out, their guns leveled at our chests. "Don't nobody move a muscle for two minutes," the last cat said. We stayed against the wall, hands raised high. In a minute we heard the sound of a car engine roaring down the street. The whole operation had lasted less than three minutes.

But we expected certain business losses like this. I had lost other money, not as spectacularly, but even larger amounts. I had lent a sister a big wad to get a beauty shop opened. I was going to be a partner and it looked like a good thing. Instead she went South with the money.

But even with the losses we had more money than we could use. Barbara and Toni no longer had to hustle. Sometimes Barbara would go out there anyhow. I would take her downtown and let her out and then come back and get her shortly before dawn. But the pressure of having to make money was gone; she was doing it just for kicks and to keep in practice.

One afternoon I saw Rat. He was still preaching with the Muslims as Bashar but since Malcolm's assassination he was not as active. He told me he was getting it on with the Black Panthers.

"Panthers ain't what a lot of dudes think they are," Rat said. "They got some good programs going. They helping cats get off drugs. Drugs burns out the brain and we need brains for the revolution."

"Tell me, man. I hear the Panthers are out to get the five Ps."

"Who's the five Ps?" Rat asked.

"Don't you know? Pigs, Prostitutes, Pimps, Pushers and Preachers. Now I ain't no preacher and I sure ain't no pig, but it's the other three that bothers me."

"Man these are just the dudes that's keeping the blacks down. Pigs are all anti-black, even the black pigs. Preachers, too. They're just playing the game and taking the black's money. Same with pimps and pushers. Man, you can understand why they gotta go, can't you?"

I saw it was useless to argue with him. "Man, Rat," I said, "you looking a little shabby around the edges. How'd you like a new suit?"

"Sure man," he said, "who's gonna get it for me?"

"Me, man," I grinned. "Your local pimp and pusher. Who else?"

"Come on, Youngblood. You don't have to buy me nothing."

"You don't want me to buy you a suit?" I said, defensively. "Maybe you don't think the kind of suit I'd buy you would be good enough?" I was surprised how easily I got on edge lately. Maybe I needed to take another cure.

Rat backed off a step. "Hey, take it easy, man. Sure I want a suit."

"Here's six bills," I said, peeling off six one hundred dollar notes. "And here's another one for shirts and that stuff." I handed him the money and walked away.

"Hey," Rat called, "thanks man. I mean really thanks."

But I wasn't hearing. I felt up tight. I needed a shot.

A week later a panic hit the city. I first learned about it from another runner named Swinger. We were having a party in a midtown hotel suite. Swinger and another big-time runner, Goldfinger, had rented the suite for three days to throw a gig. Cadillac Walter and I were invited along with some of Harlem's best jazz musicians, some gamblers, a couple of big-time numbers cats and a room full of white girls. The peephole was opened and shut often as new guests were scrutinized, then let in. Dollar pouches of coke were lying open on the table, in the kitchen, in the bathrooms. Various guests took turns rolling joints from the raw weed also spread around. Soul music came from the stereo, and the living room was dark except for the dim light which overflowed from the kitchen and hallway.

Swinger and Goldfinger seemed to be spending a lot of time in a back bedroom with some other dude I had never seen. I sat in a corner of the dim living room, smoking a reefer and snorting cocaine, which is the wildest high imaginable. Suddenly Swinger appeared in the door and motioned for me to join him in the back.

"Where's Cadillac Walter?" he said as I passed into the bedroom.

"I don't know man, I think he already left."

Swinger closed the door behind him and I could tell by the look in his eyes that something was wrong. On the table next to a pile of raw heroin was a .357 Magnum, a snub-nosed .38 and a nine-millimeter automatic. A full arsenal. Something was wrong. Bad wrong.

Goldfinger looked up from the bed where he was sitting. "A panic's on, Youngblood," he said.

I had lived through a couple of panics, but that was before I was a runner. I knew what it meant. It meant that suddenly dope was hard to find and that every junkie in the city would go crazy. It meant that addicts would be dying, but not before they killed anyone who refused to let them have dope, or money to buy it at the inflated prices.

"Who put it on?" I asked.

"It wasn't the cops, this time," Swinger said. "It is coming from our side." Heroin traffic was controlled completely by powers behind the scene—who they were guys at my level never knew. If at any time they wanted to shut off the flow they could do it until the city went into a panic. "I got the word about an hour ago," Swinger said. "It came from my controller. He said the big boys felt the price of dope was too low." Last year they had lowered the price of junk for a couple of weeks, like it was on sale. Some pushers even gave away free samples to those who wanted to try it. This time it looked like it was the other way around. "The price is going from a nickel to $7," said Swinger. "To do it they're going to pull all dope off the streets for a week. And that means a lot of cats are going to get it."

Goldfinger looked at me. "You got your piece with you?"·

"Not me, man. I don't ever carry it unless I'm in trouble."

"Well, you're in trouble now," he said.

"Hey man, what do you do in a thing like this?"

"Disappear," Swinger said. "Stay out of sight till it's all over."

He didn't have to say more. I left the party early and for two weeks never budged out of my own apartment. Even when I started going around again, the tension remained high. I didn't trust Charlie. Barbara said he'd been asking questions about my operations. Toni thought he was trying to cut in on some of the business at the whorehouse I still kept rented in Brooklyn. It was all getting on my nerves. I wanted to blame it on the drugs but I had a feeling it was something a lot deeper, that there was a hole in the inner part of my life that never had been filled, no matter how much dope and money I tried to stuff it with.

My nerves finally snapped one afternoon in a meat market near the corner of 116th and St. Nicholas.

As usual, I was stoned. A black woman was buying some pork chops. I was standing to one side, spaced out, when I saw something the woman couldn't see. The guy behind the scale had his finger on it as he weighed her meat. The woman glanced at the indicator, then opened her purse.

"Hey man," I yelled. "You're cheating that woman."

The man's face blanched and he jerked his hand away. "You're crazy, junkie."

"Don't hand me that stuff, whitey," I shouted at the top of my voice. "You think because a sister's black you get a right to take her."

"Get outta here," the man yelled back. He picked up a meat cleaver.

"Son. don't get upset," said the black woman. "It don't amount to that much anyway. Let it go."

"I'll be damned if I let it go," I said.

The butcher started around the counter, the meat cleaver in his hand. I picked up the closest thing I could find and threw it at him. It was a can of tomatoes. It glanced off his shoulder, spinning him around, making him slip on the sawdust-covered floor. He struck his head against the edge of the display case and blood began spreading over his white shirt and apron. As he struggled to get to his feet I went wild, shoving against stacks of cans and boxes, smashing bottles of juice and oil to the floor, rampaging through the store turning over shelves. Picking up a jar of olives I hurled it through the plate-glass window at the front.

I dashed out of the store and down the street, crashing into an old lady, sending her sprawling to the sidewalk. Three blocks later I turned, panting, into an alley. What was happening to me? What was wrong with my head to make me take such a risk over a few pennies that were none of my business anyway?

Even though the panic had lifted I got so I seldom left the apartment except to pick up the dope, turn over the money and sometimes deliver the junk to the street. The rest of the work I could handle by phone or leave up to Charlie. On the street I was always under surveillance either by the cops, the syndicate, or stick-up guys hoping to make a haul. One rainy Sunday morning I was supposed to make a pickup near the United Nations building. I caught a cab from

Harlem and sat in the back seat, shivering, while the driver fought the traffic down East Side Drive. The wipers smacked against the bottom of the windshield, the cab radio blared heavy rock music and inside I could feel my stomach tightening.

I told the driver to keep going as we neared the UN, to drive on down to Bellevue Hospital and let me out. There I caught another cab back up to the UN, but the feeling was still there.

I got out near the IBM building and walked across to the Plaza. My package was on a bench, soaked by the rain, waiting for me to pick it up. Again, that uneasy feeling surrounded me. I had Toad's gun in my holster, strapped to the small of my back. I knew if I were stopped by the cops with that amount of heroin in my possession, I would have to shoot it out, and something told me that if I picked up that package I'd have to.

I stood for a long time on the other side of the Plaza, looking at the rain fall in little pellets, splashing in the street, soaking the outer paper of the package on the bench. Except for the traffic coming and going, nobody was around. I stood, hunched in a doorway, the collar of my raincoat pulled up around my neck. Thirty minutes passed. The rain kept falling and the cars kept coming and going, but nobody came near the package. Yet I knew that someone else was watching that package. I felt that the minute I picked it up somebody would draw down on me and I'd have to start running and shooting. A cab came along with the roof light on and I hailed it.

As we started up First Avenue the package was still sitting on the bench—a hundred thousand dollars' worth of scag.

The next day I made one of my infrequent calls to

the controller. We went through the same process of hanging up and calling back. A strange voice answered the second time and I talked to him in the code of the street, knowing that if I were being watched outside there was the chance my phone was bugged too.

"Hey man, those tickets to the ball game yesterday weren't any good. The stadium was full. I couldn't even get close to the goal line cause there were too many spectators."

"Yeah man, we know. Sorry about that. The losing team got the ball but it's okay. We'll send you some more tickets."

So, I'd been right. The cops did have the place staked out. I felt myself starting to shake, and went into the bedroom to fix.

Two days later I ruined a quarter kilo of heroin. I was high when I cut it and instead of adding the milk and sugar first, I added the quinine. I had to pay the banker for that batch, but that didn't bother me. Money was coming in so fast from the pushers and my other business interests, that it was no problem. What worried me was that I was making mistakes.

I got extra fussy about clothes. I would buy a $300 suit, wear it once, and give it away. Sometimes I would buy a whole boxful of tailored, monogrammed dress shirts—and wear only one of them before tossing the rest. I was especially particular about shoes and would shop half a day to find just the right pair.

One of my growing anxieties was Charlie. I didn't trust him and yet I needed him to enforce the code. One Thursday noon Charlie and I visited a pusher who had been stealing from me. I pointed him out, then turned and walked away down the street. Charlie slipped on a pair of brass knucks and clobbered the guy right there on the sidewalk. I heard the dude scream and turned to see him crumple to the concrete. A black cop came racing down the sidewalk and grabbed Charlie. The cop turned to another cat who had been standing, watching. "You're a witness!"

"Buddy, I ain't no witness to nothing," the cat said. "I didn't see nothing."

"I didn't do it," Charlie said. "How come you're holding on to me? Ask the guy, he'll tell you I didn't do it." Charlie pointed to the pusher lying on the sidewalk.

The cop hauled the pusher to his feet. "Did he hit you?" The pusher looked at Charlie and then at the cop and shook his head. His mouth was torn open and his nose broken but he just shook his head. "I slipped on the sidewalk and busted my face. He was trying to help me."

Charlie grinned and walked away.

At the trick house on Bergen Street in Brooklyn, I had an old wino on my payroll. He'd sit at the base of the stairs and collect the fees from the prostitutes who used the place. It was a thriving business. Half of the money went to the landlord and the other half to me (that is, after the wino cheated us out of his cut). But Charlie was muscling in, collecting from the wino himself. As much as I needed him for protection, I began to look for some way to set him up for an accident.

But I didn't have to. One of Cadillac Walter's girls got to him first. Charlie tried to pull her, thinking, no doubt, that it was time he went into business for himself. When she laughed at him he lost his cool and slapped her around. She waited until he turned his back and then came at him with a broken Coke bottle.

But it left me wide open, without protection. I didn't regret Charlie's death, but I knew mine couldn't be long in coming.

15

JESUS COMES TO HARLEM

> *It's me,*
> *It's me, O Lord,*
> *Standin' in the need of*
> *prayer.*
> —Negro Spiritual

So THIS was what brought me to that hot summer night, standing on 125th Street, listening to the jangling music, feeling alone. I needed a fix. Bad.

"I've been watching you, Youngblood," the little Puerto Rican had said. "God has His hand on your life and wants to change you."

I knew better. Christianity was a white man's religion. But the jerk wouldn't let me alone. "God has spoken to me," he said. "He said to tell you He is going to change your life."

I turned and moved on down the sidewalk.

Ten blocks later, I turned into the shooting gallery on 116th Street. I locked myself in a back room and mixed the huge overdose. I knew what I was doing, but it seemed to be the only way to escape. I thought over what had led me to this moment; the emptiness of all I reached for once I got it, the hour by hour danger I lived with, the feel of my body decaying

Why not meet death on my own terms, not screaming in some stinking cell or at the hands of another hustler somewhere?

I shook out the white powder in the spoon, poured a little water into it from a jar on the table and mixed it with the end of my finger. I pulled out my gold cigarette lighter, snapped the flame and held it under the spoon. The mixture began to boil. Picking up the medicine dropper-hypo, I squeezed the rubber bulb and then released it, slowly drawing the fluid into the needle. Finally I inserted the needle into the mainline.

Immediately I felt the rush in my stomach. I knew I had killed myself. I tried to get up but I couldn't move, I was dying, I felt my body go rigid. Fear swept over me. Every muscle was paralyzed. I could feel my heart slowing down, my lungs straining against ribs that would not move.

Yet I did not die. Something was in that room with me. Some kind of breath or—Presence—seemed to join me; it surrounded me, it hovered over me.

I sat there, dead but conscious, for many hours, and the invisible thing stayed with me. Then, almost imperceptibly, my heartbeat picked up. Feeling returned, I moved a hand.

I staggered out of the shooting gallery into the street. It was early Sunday morning. Like a sleepwalker I turned toward my apartment. I had killed myself but I wasn't dead. Why?

A few days later, Toni got busted. Toni had been jailed before and it was always an easy matter to spring her. But this time she made a big mistake, and it was going to cost her. A cop had conned her into selling him some heroin, then busted her.

I knew I was going to have to get a lawyer, but it was late at night when I heard. I'd have to wait until morning. A good attorney would cost us a couple of grand and her bail could run as high as ten thousand on this case, depending on whether they were going to try to stick her or not. But we shouldn't have any trouble, or at least that's what I thought.

Early the next morning the telephone rang. "Uh, yeah, who it is?" I mumbled into the receiver.

"Pick up the Dooley at Fourth and Dean in Brooklyn," the voice said. "Our man knows you. Be there at ten this morning."

Suddenly I was awake. The voice sounded unfamiliar. "Hey man, run that by again," I said. "Ten o'clock where?"

"Fourth and Dean," the voice said, irritated, and there was a sharp click on the other end of the line.

I leaned over and picked up my wristwatch on the nightstand. It was 8:30 a.m. By the time I had shaved and dressed it was 9:15. Barbara was still sound asleep as I gave the finishing tug to my tie. It was a tie that Toni had bought for me the week before at Saks Fifth Avenue. I'd contact the attorney as soon as I got back. Toni's habit was almost as big as mine now and she'd be climbing those walls.

I was worried. Something about that phone call sounded fishy. I took Toad's gun from the drawer in the nightstand and slung it on my back. Then, foolishly, I taped a small bundle of heron to the inside of my calf, thinking I would use the trip to Brooklyn to make a quick delivery as well.

I caught a cab in front of my hotel and by ten was standing leisurely on the corner at Fourth and Dean in South Brooklyn. All I had to do now was wait.

Suddenly I heard a car screech around the corner. I looked up. The car braked in front of me. Four men with guns in their hands came barreling out.

"Don't move, Johnson," one of them said, pointing the muzzle of his gun in my face. It was Watusi.

I froze. "You guys come on like gangbusters," I said.

"Up against the wall, nigger," Watusi said, grabbing me by the shoulder and spinning me around. "Hands over your head and feet apart. Now lean."

I stood there, face to the building, while they ran their hands over me. The first thing they found was my gun. The cop grabbed the tails of my coat and pulled them apart, ripping the coat up the seam. He pulled the gun from its hidden holster.

Then he felt my legs. "Here it is, Sarge." Again I heard the rip of cloth as he tore my trousers open from the cuff to the knee and yanked the plastic-wrapped package roughly away from my skin. "Looks like a bundle."

I turned and looked at the sullen crowd which had already gathered. "Police brutality!" I shouted. "I ain't done nothing."

There was a low murmur from the crowd of blacks that ringed the action.

Watusi turned and looked at the faces. "Back up," he snarled.

Slowly the ring of people moved back. "It looks like you'd be out chasing criminals rather than picking on a nice young man like that," an old woman muttered as one of the cops gestured her backwards.

Moments later my hands were yanked behind my back and I felt the hard, cold metal of handcuffs being clamped around them. I was shoved into the police car. We moved away from the curb as Watusi, sitting beside the driver, made his report on the radio.

Finishing, he turned around. "Your luck has run out, Youngblood," he said. "You're going to have a long time to come off your high—like 15 years."

But it wasn't the 15-year sentence that worried me right then, it was the three days just ahead. I was going to have to go cold turkey again. They booked me at the 79th Precinct, then took me to Old Queens Prison to await trial.

I was thrown into a cell on the third tier. The tiny room had two cots suspended from the walls with chains. There was no privacy; the small barred window looked down on a courtyard, but the front was completely open with only iron bars separating it from the walkway high above the ground floor. The only furniture beside the cots was an open toilet without a seat. The combined stench of disinfectant and urine was overpowering.

My cellmate was an old dope fiend I had seen on the streets. Toothless and almost bald, he had been using heroin for more years than I was old. He told me that more than two-thirds of his forty years had been spent in reform schools, jails and prisons. Yet the moment he was released he always went right back to dope. Fortunately for me he knew what it was like to have to kick cold turkey, so when they clanged the door shut behind me he let me alone. There would be time enough to talk after I had been to hell and back.

I had tried to call Barbara from the precinct office, but no one answered in our apartment. I fought down the feeling of panic, convincing myself that it wouldn't take long for the word to get around that I was in jail. Barbara would bail me out. But where was she?

That night I sat on the edge of my bunk bracing myself, waiting for the pain. Waiting for the running nose, the cramps, the nausea, the diarrhea and finally the convulsions which could lead to insanity.

Down the long row of cells I could hear the men

talking, laughing. My stomach cramped some and I bent over, gritting my teeth and waiting for the full force to hit me. Instead, the cramping eased and I sat up, puzzled. About 4 a.m., as I finished the last of my cigarettes, I again had that uncanny feeling of something or someone standing close to me—like in the shooting gallery the week before. There was a Presence in the cell that I sensed rather than saw. It was a warm glow, a sensation that I could feel hovering around my skin, like it was all over me and inside me too.

When dawn broke, the sensation was still there. I had not experienced any pain. My cellmate looked at me sharply. "How'd you get dope in here, man!"

"I haven't any dope," I answered.

"Ain't you got a habit?"

"That's right."

"How bad?"

"Dealer's."

"Then how come you ain't screaming your lungs out? You gotta have some dope on you and I want some."

"Listen, old man, if I had some dope I'd be taking it myself. I haven't got any."

Why hadn't I gone into violent withdrawal?

The end of the second day I was able to get the word to a dude who was being released to call Barbara and tell her I needed help. Moment by moment I expected to start withdrawing and the longer I waited, the greater became the suspense. The dude promised to make the call the minute he walked out and I returned to my hunched-over position on the bed, waiting for hell to break loose in my guts. Instead, all I felt was that strange sensation. It was as though someone had breathed all over me and the breath lingered, sticking to my skin like an invisible cloud.

The third day, and still no word from Barbara. By this time I was in a daze. I had gone without food, thinking it would be easier on me when the nausea struck. But still there were no withdrawal symptoms, and still that Presence hovered around me. I had apparently kicked cold turkey without any effects.

Sometime during the third night the Presence left me. I was awakened the next morning by a guard banging on the bars of the cell. "We're taking you down to court in an hour, Johnson," he said.

I stood while the judge mechanically read the indictment and called for the lab report—the collected evidence that had been gathered against me.

But the report seemed to be missing. The judge called for Watusi, as arresting officer, but he was absent. I was surprised. I knew how long he had looked forward to this and wondered what kept him away. The judge sent me back to my cell to be recalled in a week. Surely, I thought, Barbara will show up before then.

But the week dragged by with no word from her. The next Monday morning I was taken to court again. Again the judge called for the evidence and the arresting officer. Both were still missing. Angry, the judge again had me returned to my cell. By this time I was a puppet on a string. When the guards said walk, I walked. When they said sit, I sat. All my actions seemed to have been prearranged long ago and I had no choice but to follow after.

Monday morning of the third week I stood again before the judge's bench. After reading the indictment he looked up and said, "This man's been here twice before. Where is the arresting officer?"

I turned and looked over the courtroom. Watusi

was nowhere to be seen. The judge turned to the prosecutor. "All right, let's hear the evidence against him."

The prosecutor shrugged his shoulders. "I'm sorry, your Honor, but the lab report is missing also. I don't know what happened."

I was puzzled. Was it some kind of a trick? But the judge sounded genuinely upset. "What's going on here?" he roared. "This man has been accused of a felony and this is the third time he's appeared before this bench without evidence against him. You know what that means in the State of New York!"

The young prosecutor blinked. "I'm sorry, your Honor, but we're prosecuting more than 50 cases a day. Something just got fouled up."

The judge looked over the bench and with rage and frustration said to me, "You're a menace to every decent citizen, Johnson. If I had my way I'd lock you up forever. But the laws of the State of New York say that if you appear before this bench three times without evidence I have to turn you loose."

Squeezing his lips together he banged the gavel on the top of the desk and motioned for the guards to escort me out. Minutes later I stood blinking in the sunlight outside the courtroom.

Suddenly all the strangeness fell into place. Barbara. Watusi. The lab report. My release. It *is* a trick, I thought. They're going to follow me to find who my controller is. Maybe they got to Barbara and she ratted.

I walked quickly away and caught the first subway back to Manhattan. I changed trains three times and finally came up in Grand Central Station. Leaving the subway I sauntered through the crowds to the street where I hailed a cab. I stayed with the cab two blocks and then got out on the corner of Fifth Avenue and 43rd, walked a block and sat down on the steps of the New York Public Library.

The sun felt good and I leaned back, absorbing its warmth, while through half-closed eyes I scanned the sidewalk to see if I had been followed. The coast seemed clear but then another thought, even more frightening, clutched my mind.

The syndicate! How could I convince them I had not made a deal with the cops? I, myself, didn't understand why I was free. How could I ever convince my suppliers that I hadn't turned stoolie? If I had to choose between the two, I would much rather have the cops after me than the Mafia—at least the cops don't use piano wire around your throat in the middle of the night.

I checked again to see if I was followed, then caught the Lexington Avenue IRT up to 125th and quickly made my way to my hotel-apartment. I had more than 50 grand worth of heroin stashed there that hadn't been delivered to my pushers. There was a lot of cash, I didn't know how much, stuffed into drawers and that clothes hamper in the bathroom. Thinking as I walked, I planned to grab as many dollars as I could carry and catch a plane to Puerto Rico—anywhere—until things cooled off. With either the cops or the Mafia after me—or maybe both—I had no choice but to run.

In the parking lot beside the hotel were the pimpmobiles—pink Caddys, polka-dot Lincolns, custom-made Continentals and my own gold Caddy with the leopard-skin top. The lobby was filled with hustlers: pimps, numbers runners, dope pushers and prostitutes. I walked quickly through, speaking to no one, and straight up the stairs. I'd flush the heroin, grab some money and clothes, and run.

Standing in front of the door I paused, listening, looking in both directions. No one in sight. Only the soft whish of tires outside and the occasional dim honk of a horn filtered through the window at the end of the hall. I put the key in the lock and opened the door. But before I could step across the threshold, I heard a voice.

"Turn around," it said.

Startled, I whirled around. No one was there. I stood frozen in the half-open doorway.

"Turn around," the voice persisted. It seemed to come from without and yet at the same time from within me. My fingers curled tightly around the doorknob. Inside was my life. The suits, the cash, the dope—heaven and hell, freedom and slavery—all mixed together like powdered sugar and heroin.

I felt the knob grow slick in my hand as sweat formed in my palm. What was happening to me?

"Turn around," the voice repeated, gently.

"Where will I go?" I argued desperately.

"Come to Me, Aaron," said the voice.

Like a man in a dream I turned and started slowly down the corridor. I left the door ajar, the key in the lock. I walked down the stairs. The lobby was full of old friends.

"Hey Youngblood, when did you get out?"

But I looked neither right nor left as I walked through the ornate front door and out on the sidewalk. The sun was blinding. My Cadillac was in the lot, but I passed it by. The light seemed to grow brighter until I could barely see. On down the street I walked. Block by block, still in a dream.

I didn't know where I was going, only that I could not go back. The sun blazed on my squinted eyelids as I groped from one lamppost to the next. Where was I supposed to go? And then I remembered something Aunt Rose had said.

"You can always go to the Neals'."

16

PLAY IT COOL, BABY

It's the best I can do.
I learned all my Christianity
from white folks.
—James Baldwin

"AARON!" said Mrs. Neal as she opened the door of her apartment. "Come on in, child." She didn't act like she was at all surprised to see me.

The soft twilight of the living room eased the pain of my aching eyes. "Mrs. Neal, I need help."

"I know, son. Your Aunt Rose told me all about it before she and Arthur left. I'm glad you've come here. Sit down."

"You don't understand," I said.

"Yes, I do. You're addicted."

"It isn't that," I said. "I'm not sure what it is, but it's not that." Then I told her about going cold turkey in jail without any pain, and about the voice outside my apartment—and how I'd just walked away without even closing the door.

"Sounds to me like the Lord has His hand on you," she said, her eyes moist and her fat little face quivering with excitement.

The Lord? That was the same word the little Puerto Rican dude had used. . . .

176

"But I don't know anything about any 'Lord.'"

"That don't make no difference," Mrs. Neal said, pulling up her apron and wiping her eyes. "The Lord knows you. Didn't He call you by name there by your apartment door?"

Mrs. Neal was short and plump, her head barely coming up to my chest. But reaching up, she put her hands on my shoulders. "Let me tell you something, son. I been praying for you ever since you came out of the army on drugs. Your Aunt Rose used to come around here from the beauty shop and sit right there on that old sofa and I'd pray with her. And ever since then I've been praying for you every day."

"But you don't even know me, Mrs. Neal."

"Sure, I know you. I've knowed you from a boy. You just didn't know me. It's just like you and the Lord. He knows all about you, it's just you don't know Him. Now He's called you."

"But what do I do?"

"Fast and pray, son, fast and pray."

I stared at her. "Fast? I'm not trying to be disrespectful, ma'm, but what are you talking about?"

Mrs. Neal walked over to her table and picked up a battered flop-edged Bible. "Aaron, this book is all about God's Son. Now when Jesus wanted to find out what God was saying to Him while He was here on earth, He fasted. That means going without food. He also prayed. You know what that means, don't you?"

I nodded my head.

Mrs. Neal pointed to a door opening off the living room. "Just you take that room and stay as long as you like, fasting and praying."

"You mean I can just go in there and talk to God, even if I don't know who He is?"

"Mostly listen, Aaron. You talk if you want to, but true prayer is mostly listening."

The room was very small. There was a single iron bed, and a wooden table, the green paint chipping off. And there was a creaky wooden chair with a thin gray mat tied to the seat with twine. A mirror, chipped around the edges, hung on the wall. A shallow closet, just deep enough to hang a suit sidewise, was beside the door. Across the room, beyond the bed, was a window. Through the dirt-streaked glass I could see a brick wall of the next apartment building.

I closed the door behind me and pulled the string on the bare bulb, which dangled from the ceiling. I sat down on the side of the bed, feeling the springs sag beneath my weight. How many times had I sat on the edge of just such a bed in just such a room and rolled up my sleeve—the works beside me? Now the only thing beside me was the dog-eared Bible Mrs. Neal had handed me and, strangely, there was no desire for a fix. None.

I sat in the gloom, listening to the silence around me. And slowly I became aware again of that Presence, hovering around me. Closer—as though it clothed every cell in my body. Into my mind came an urge to pick up the book and read it. I laid it in my lap, feeling the worn, frayed leather cover with my fingers. I let it drop open in the middle and began to read the unfamiliar words:

> *God is our refuge and strength, a very present help in trouble. Therefore will not we fear, though the earth be removed and though the mountains be carried into the midst of the sea; though the waters thereof roar and be troubled, though the mountains shake with the swelling thereof. . . . the Lord of hosts is with us; the God of Jacob is our refuge. . . . Be still and know that I am*

> *God: I will be exalted among the heathen,*
> *I will be exalted in the earth.*

Raising my head from the book I spoke to Him for the first time in all my life. "Lord ... Lord of hosts ... This is Youngblood ..."

Both inside me and out I seemed to hear the voice. "Your name is Aaron."

I tried again, "God ... God of Jacob ... This is Aaron."

Something was happening. I felt my eyes filling with tears and overflowing. I had cried many times before. Junkies cry a lot. Your eyes burn and sting, your nose waters, but this was different. This time there was a deep ache in my chest but not a bad ache. The tears fell down my face, splashing on the Bible in my lap.

What was happening to me? But even as I asked the question the answer came, again both from within and without. "For cleansing. Tears are my rivers of cleansing."

"Lord ..." I stammered again, "Lord ..."

I dug at my eyes with both hands and looked back at the book in my lap. Through the blur of tears my eyes fell on another verse on the same page:

> *If we have forgotten the name of our God,*
> *or stretched out our hands to a strange God;*
> *shall not God search this out? for he*
> *knoweth the secrets of the heart.*

Suddenly I was on the floor beside the bed, my face buried in the faded quilt, my body quivering with sobs. I didn't understand it, I didn't care. All I knew was that some way God was cleaning me out.

For three days I remained in that room, coming out

only to get a cup of coffee and talk briefly with Mrs. Neal. But mostly I stayed in the room with the light out and the door closed. I felt my body changing. Even though I was not eating I felt myself growing stronger. And my thoughts were changing. Once I tried to force myself to think about dope, about my car, about money . . . but there was no desire.

On the fourth night I was on my knees beside the chair. It felt good to talk to Him, even though I really didn't know anything about Him, even His name. Mrs. Neal and the Puerto Rican called Him "the Lord." But apparently He was also called Jehovah, or God of Jacob, or God Almighty, or Jesus.

Kneeling there beside the chair, my head in my hands, I was suddenly aware of a light in the room behind me—and the sensation of someone standing there. Mrs. Neal must have opened the door very quietly. I didn't really want to talk to anyone, yet this was her house and I owed her so much. Straightening up on my knees, I looked back.

The door was closed, the room empty. But a light was there. It was a strange light, without any source. It had form, an indescribable form that was neither round nor flat, not like a man yet not like a thing either. The light seemed to hover in the middle of the room, between me and the door.

And all at once I knew! It was the Presence—the Presence from the shooting gallery, from the prison, from the hall in the hotel. It was Jesus. The Puerto Rican's Jesus. Mrs. Neal's Jesus. He was the Lord of Hosts, the God of Jacob, Jehovah. He was the same.

Almost involuntarily I felt my hands stretching up over my head while from the depths of my self came strange, fluent, beautiful sounds. They sounded like words, only I couldn't understand a one of them. It was as if a river was pouring out of somewhere deep inside, only it was a river of love and thanks and gratitude. I don't know how long this lasted. Far into the night, I think. The next thing I remember was the sun reflecting off the brick wall outside the window. I was stretched out on the floor where I had spent the night in praise.

That morning I told Mrs. Neal about my strange experience. "Honey," she said, heading for the refrigerator to bring out bacon and eggs. "It sounds to me like it's time for you to eat again."

Mrs. Neal (who now insisted I call her Sister Neal) said that the sounds I had made the night before were called "speaking in tongues." It was prayer, she said. After breakfast, when we prayed together, the beautiful musiclike words of praise came again. Sister Neal urged me to go around to a place called The Church of God in Christ and talk to the pastor, Bishop Clemmons.

Once, when I was a small boy, Aunt Rose had put on a fashion show at the big Bethany Baptist Church in Brooklyn. The ladies of the church were trying to raise money for their pastor's vacation and Aunt Rose had taken me along to help model for her. Except for this time, I had never been inside a church building in my life.

Now I made my way through the unfamiliar gloom of the church and found the pastor's office, located deep in a maze of the dark corridors. Bishop Clemmons greeted me cordially and, after calling in his sons who assisted him in the ministry, he listened to my story with great interest. He admitted, frankly, that he knew very little about drug addiction. However, he said, there was an organization in Brooklyn known as Teen Challenge which helped drug addicts find God. He recommended I contact them.

Walking out of the ill-lit building I stood for a moment blinking in the late afternoon sun. As I turned down the sidewalk toward Sister Neal's apartment I heard a car purring along the curb next to me. Glancing over I saw a sleek Lincoln Continental. A chauffeur sat stonefaced behind the wheel. I knew only one man who had a chauffeur-driven Continental: Goldfinger.

The back window next to the curb swished down. The dope dealer was sitting well back in the seat. I leaned down as the car came to a stop.

Goldfinger talked quickly, chewing on his cigar at the same time. "Hey baby, you all right?"

I grinned, embarrassed, and said, "Sure man, everything's fine."

"People been asking about you. When you coming back to Harlem?"

"I'm not coming back," I said. "I've been doing a lot of thinking and some things been happening in my life. I'm getting out of the game."

Goldfinger made no commitments. "Whatever you say, baby," he said, taking his cigar out of his mouth and glancing out the back window. "But play it cool, baby, with a soft beat. There's a contract out on you."

My mouth suddenly dried. I straightened up away from the window of the car. Goldfinger nodded, ever so slightly. The car slid into traffic, the electric window gliding back into place at the same time.

A contract. Had I forgotten that a man never walks off from the Mafia? Suddenly it was like before. I looked wildly up and down the street. Any one of those people could be a hired gun, paid to kill me. I wanted to run. I wanted to dash back inside the church building. I wanted to jump behind a closed door and stay there. Instead I made myself walk slowly, deliberately, all the way back to Sister Neal's. But once inside I ran to my room, grabbed the Bible, and fell across the bed. Only here, in this place where I had first known Jesus, did I feel safe.

Three days later I was in the back of a Volkswagen bus bouncing across the Pennsylvania countryside toward the Teen Challenge farm at Rherersburg. I had gone to the headquarters of this group of Christians who were helping young people put the power of the Holy Spirit to work in their lives. They greeted me warmly and when I told them my story, agreed that it would be best for me to get out of the city until things cooled off, and also until I could receive some basic Bible training. They planned to take a group of addicts down to their farm and arrangements were made to have me along.

For the first time since I'd left Aunt Rose's, I came face-to-face with a disciplined life: getting up at a certain time, eating meals at a certain time, performing chores on the farm. At the end of the first week I was baptized in water. Whatever · doubts I may have had about this new way of life were all buried that day. I came up from the baptismal waters knowing that even if this future held death at the hands of a Mafia gun, there was no turning back—ever.

After a month of Bible study and discipline in prayer and submission, the leaders at the farm asked me if I would be willing to go with one of their men on a trip to Ohio. The idea was to go into various churches and schools to promote the work of Teen Challenge. Since I was the only black at the farm, they felt it would be good to have me go along and share my testimony.

We were gone for almost a month, traveling all across Ohio. Over and over again I stood before groups of people, all kinds of people, and told what had happened to me. I spoke in small Pentecostal churches that had never had a black person enter the door. I spoke in all-black high schools. I spoke to little old ladies who had never heard the word "junkie," and I spoke in jails where everyone present was a drug addict. On several occasions we went into the ghettos of the larger cities and set up microphones and loudspeakers on the street corners and testified to anybody who'd listen.

Three months after my conversion I returned to New York, with two white ex-addicts from Teen Challenge. Elihu and Roger and I were going to try talking to addicts in Harlem. I was nervous as I helped Roger and Elihu set up loudspeakers on the corner of 112th and Seventh—surely someone would recognize me. But we might as well have been in Cleveland, for the people who passed by were all strangers.

Elihu stood in front of the microphone and sang a few songs. A small crowd gathered and then Roger did a little preaching. Finally he called me to come forward and speak. I started to tell what had happened in my life but before I had gotten far I was interrupted by a shout.

"Hey Youngblood! You got a new game going?"

Someone else laughed. Now the whole corner was filled with laughing black faces. It was hopeless. The mood was ruined; the meeting was over.

Roger and Elihu and I started putting the sound equipment back in the bus. Kneeling down and wrapping a loudspeaker cord around the base of a speaker I suddenly noticed a pair of flashy white and brown shoes beside me. Before I could glance up from my crouched position I felt a hard, blunt instrument against the back of my head.

"Freeze!" a voice said softly.

I froze.

"Bang!" the voice said. Then it broke out in a laugh. "Hey Youngblood, h-h-how's it g-g-going?"

It was Rat, standing over me with his cakecutter in his hand, laughing like he was going to die.

It took me long seconds to recover.

"Man," I sighed, standing up, "don't ever do that."

Rat snickered. "H-H-How's it with you b-b-baby. This a pretty good g-g-game?" Rat's stuttering was back, and worse than I had ever known it. He seemed to be fighting to get each word out of his mouth.

"No man, this ain't no game. This is for real. I'm through with the game. This is for life and death."

"M-M-Man, the last I heard of you old Watusi had finally busted you good and they were ready to throw the k-k-key away. You ain't playing pigeon with the fuzz, are you baby?"

"No way, baby," I said shaking my head. "It's all Jesus. He got me out of jail. He took away my addiction. He did it all."

Rat stared at me, then at the other ex-addicts who were loading the stuff in the Volks. "L-L-Listen man, I gotta get some help. The monkey's on my back again and it's about to kill me."

"I thought you were working with the Panthers," I said.

"Naw, that was just another g-g-game. They're trying to help people, but with them it's kill, kill, kill. Man, what I need is some life."

I put my hand on his shoulder. "Didn't you hear what Roger just finished saying? You know what to do."

"Man, how can I turn my life over to Jesus? I don't even know who Jesus is."

"Jesus is God, Rat," I said, looking deep into his

eyes. Rat couldn't hold the look. He cast his eyes down.

"Dammit," I said excitedly. "Stop looking every place else! Look in my eyes. You see any dope there? You see any broads there?"

Rat forced himself to look. "No," he said.

I had him by both shoulders now. "What do you see?"

He paused, then said softly, "Man, it's like I can see all the way through you."

"That's what Jesus does for you. No more dark glasses. No more fogged-out brain. I'm a new man."

"B-B-But what about me?" Rat said.

"If you ask Him, God will change your life too."

I was thinking, I guess, of a private place off somewhere, like at Sister Neal's. But before I could stop him, Rat was down on his knees right on the sidewalk.

Elihu and Roger quickly put down the equipment and joined me. We made a circle around Rat. "Lord Jesus," Roger prayed, "save our brother from junk and set him free."

A crowd was gathering again. Unlike the crowd of a few moments before, these cats were quiet. They were looking. Listening. The corner of 112th Street and Seventh Avenue was filled with a kind of reverence. I sensed the hunger of Harlem, the desire of my brothers to be set free from all that binds them.

Rat was getting to his feet. He glanced at the faces around him and then began to cry. Roger kept urging him to come down to the Teen Challenge Center with us, but he wouldn't. At last I gave him a card with the phone number on it. "Call me, Rat, tonight or tomorrow."

Rat did call, but it was a week later. In the meantime he had shot himself full of dope. But there was a difference. This time, he said, he wasn't able to get high. It was like shooting water. Nothing happened. At the end of the week he stopped shooting altogether.

"I'm finished," he said when he called. "I ain't got the hunger anymore. I don't understand it, man, but I'm clean."

There was something else I noticed about Rat. He had stopped stuttering again. I never did ask him about it and he never mentioned it, but it was gone. However, when I suggested we get together in Harlem and rap about things he backed off.

"Uh, hey man. I don't think you ought to come back over here."

"How come. What do you mean?"

"The word's out, you know."

"What word?"

"That contract out on you. I don't think you ought to come back until things cool off."

"Man, things like that never cool off. If they want to kill me, they will. What can I do about it?"

"Listen, man, these cats ain't fooling. Last week they got Goldfinger."

My heart almost stopped beating and I felt that old familiar fear clutching at my guts. I couldn't speak.

"Hey, Aaron," Rat called out into the phone. "You still there?"

"Yeah, baby, I'm here. What's this about Goldfinger?"

"It's the biggest burn in Harlem since they got Malcolm in the Audubon Ballroom."

"No man, I can't believe it. What happened?"

"No one knows for sure. But someone gave old Goldfinger the O.D. of all O.D.s. They found him in the back seat of his Continental way over in Jersey, shot full of horse mixed with arsenic."

"Jesus . . ." I whispered into the phone.

"So man, ' I were you I'd either go south or go to the top and beg them cats to pull the contract. Otherwise you're a dead man."

I was scheduled to "give my testimony" next day at Washington Temple, one of the largest black churches in Brooklyn. It was an old theatre converted into a church auditorium and it was always packed. I would be a perfect target there.

"Lord," I prayed that night when I slipped to my knees beside the bed, "I've given my life to You and I guess it doesn't make much sense for me to get worried about these cats out to kill me. After all, my life is Yours now and if they take it they gotta take it from You, not from me. Just help me tomorrow to preach like a dying man to dying men."

The next morning I stood on the platform, outfitted in a long black robe with velvet lapels. Maybe it was the robe. Maybe it was the pulpit, the church building, the organ. Maybe it was that crowd of more than a thousand blacks singing, clapping their hands, shouting "Amen," swaying in unison to the music. Maybe it was the answer to my prayer. For whatever reason, that morning I found my tongue.

"As long as I can remember I been playing the game," I said. "I've stood on street corners talking slick out of the side of my mouth so folks would think I'm hip. I've played numbers, robbed stores, sold smack, worked prostitutes. I've done it all. I was on heroin for five years. I had a dealer's habit. I thought that dropping reds, smoking pot, tripping on LSD and shooting horse was where it was at. But something happened to me. And this morning I want to tell you that the only thing that's real is Jesus Christ."

The audience, made up mostly of young faces, was with me.

"Preach it, man!" they shouted.

I continued. "Jesus alone saves. He sets you free, man, he sets you free from dope and sin."

Shouts of approval. I forgot all about the fear that some gun might be out there. My voice rose. "I watched an 11-year-old boy shooting heroin outside my apartment last week ... his mother was an addict ... his father in the penitentiary ... because of heroin ... he was only 11 ... but he looked 20 ..."

In between each sentence the people were shouting as the story gained pitch. "When I saw him fix heroin in his vein ... when he told me he had been shooting for six months ... I began to cry. That's right ... I began to cry ... and right then ... I gave my life to God all over again ... I made a vow to do everything I could to get drugs out of the ghetto ... somebody told me the Mafia has a contract out on me ... they think I'm ratting to the police ... well, I ain't ratting to no police ... I'm rapping about Jesus."

The shouts of "Amen" echoed across the auditorium.

I preached that morning for more than an hour and when I finished the organist began to play as the people shouted and clapped. One by one at first, then by the dozens, people came pouring down the aisle and knelt at the altar. I couldn't believe it. Young kids were crying, reaching in their pockets and throwing needles, spoons, pills, joints, up on the stage and then collapsing at the altar in tears. It was the happiest moment of my life.

It was later, as I left the church by a side door, that I saw her. She was waiting for me on the sidewalk.

"Barbara!"

She was living, she said, in an apartment on the other side of Brooklyn. On the subway she filled me in on what had happened the day I was arrested. She had awakened to find me gone. This was nothing unusual; she supposed I had gone to contact the lawyer for Toni. She got dressed and caught a cab to the Port Authority building where she was to meet one of her regular customers. While waiting on the corner she was picked up by a rookie cop, a gung-ho type, on a charge of loitering with the intent to prostitute. Barbara was locked up. Usually Toni or I would have bailed her out in a couple of hours. But Toni was in jail and although Barbara didn't know it, I was at that very moment being booked in Brooklyn. It seemed hard to believe that all three of us would be picked up at the same time in different parts of the huge city. Toni, Barbara said, was still in jail, doing three years in women's prison.

As the subway rocked along, I tried to find out what it meant, Barbara coming to church. It turned out she'd heard about me speaking and simply come to see me. I tried to tell her about what was happening in my life, but it was like I was talking a foreign language. She was outlawing, prostituting without a pimp, and looked bad. On the street a girl can grow old in one night, if she doesn't have a pimp to take care of her.

Once inside the apartment she went straight to the kitchen cabinet, got out a bottle of vodka, and poured herself a drink. She poured another and handed it to me.

"No. Look, Barbara. You don't understand. I don't drink anymore. I don't shoot stuff or snort coke."

She stood there looking at me a long while, then swallowed the drink. "Baby, are you for real? I thought you was just into some other game."

I gave her a half grin. "So does everybody else. But I just don't need it anymore."

"Damn," Barbara said, drinking my drink now. "Everything is changing too fast for me. You were the one nigger I dreamed about when I was in jail, and now you're running the church game."

"Baby," I said, "this is the one thing in my life that's for real."

"Yeah," Barbara said. She lit a cigarette and crossed the room to the sofa. Flopping, she kicked off her shoes. "When I heard you was gonna be there in that church this morning I just had to come."

"And that was the only reason you came? To see me?" I asked.

She looked strangely at me. "What do you mean? Sure that was the reason." She dropped her eyes and stared at the cigarette in her hand.

I sat down near her. "Hey, listen baby. You trying to pull one on Youngblood? I know you better than that. I know you better than any man in the world."

Barbara ground the cigarette out in an overflowing ashtray. Seconds later she was in my arms, her head buried in my shoulder. "God I've missed you. You are my man, my man."

I stroked her hair. "I feel something special about you too, baby," I said. "But you've got to believe me when I say that every need in my life has been met."

"You're getting me confused," she said, shaking her head against my chest. "I don't understand this talk."

I pulled her arms loose from around my neck and stood up. "Barbara! Get out of the game! You're a beautiful girl, but you're beginning to go. I mean, what is out there, in the future? Nothing!"

Barbara looked up at me. "Youngblood, I'm in big trouble. I got a baby coming and I don't want to think about it. I keep hoping it'll go away, but I know it won't. You and me we could buy a house over in Jersey. When the bread is down I could come back and hook awhile ..."

I was shaking my head. She smiled grimly and gave a tiny shrug. "I should have known. There's not a man in the world that really cares when a girl needs him."

"I love you, Barbara," I said softly. "But in a different way."

"Listen man, don't come in here with a line like that."

"I mean it. Youngblood is dead."

"Man, you've really flipped out," Barbara said, getting up to pour another drink. "You sound like Rat when he got on that Muslim jag."

Rat's changed too," I said. "He accepted Jesus and now he's working with a Christian rehabilitation group that takes in ex-cons and ..."

Barbara was back in my arms, her lips against mine. I kissed her back briefly.

"That was good-by," I said, pushing myself away. "I'm not strong enough to argue very long with you, baby. I've gotta split."

Barbara reached out for me. "No, baby, don't go. I'm sorry. I didn't mean to try to turn you on. Don't leave. I need you. I've got big trouble."

"Barbara, if money will help, I'll get a job. You'll never have to work again. Only I can't stay with you."

She came at me full force, grabbing me about the

neck. "Don't leave me, Blood. Be my man again. Please don't leave me."

She hadn't heard a thing I'd said. I untangled myself and backed to the door. "I gotta go, baby. I can't touch you no more."

Barbara reached down and picked up the vodka glass as I opened the hall door. "You son-of-a-bitchin'-con-man! I'll kill you!" She threw the glass, smashing it out in the hall. Her face was screwed in anger.

I ducked out, pulling the door behind me just as the vodka bottle smashed against it. On the street I hailed a cab and collapsed in the back seat. My hands were shaking as I reached for a cigarette. Then, remembering I didn't smoke anymore, I closed my eyes and began to pray.

If God had reached me, surely He could reach Barbara. For the time being all I knew was that I was far too weak, far too new, far too inexperienced to be His servant for this particular task.

17

LET MY PEOPLE GO

> *Go tell it on the mountain,*
> *Over the hill and everywhere,*
> *Go tell it on the mountain,*
> *To let my people go.*
>   —Appalachian folk song

BISHOP CLEMMONS of the Church of God in Christ encouraged me to enroll in Northwest Bible College in Edmonton, Alberta, Canada. But I was confused. Undecided. There were too many loose ends dangling in my life. Rat was doing great, serving with a Christian group that ministered to ex-prisoners. Barbara, I knew better than to try to influence just now. But there was Toni. Ever since Barbara told me where she was I'd been trying to get permission to visit—just to see her, to beg her forgiveness, to try to make amends in some tiny way for what I had done. But one look at my own record and prison authorities automatically turned down my request.

And, of course, the longest ache in my heart was Aunt Rose. Somehow, some way, I had to find her, to tell her that maybe her years of care were not wasted, that maybe I was still going to turn out someone she could be proud of.

Meanwhile, Teen Challenge was sending a group

down to Washington to set up a center in the D.C. area. Washington is more than 50 percent black, so it seemed like a natural idea for me to go along.

It was there, during the three months I was in Washington, that my mind was opened to the whole bag of race prejudice. It wasn't directed at me; I was seemingly accepted every place I went. It was directed toward local blacks who were being won to Christ in our preaching campaigns.

One of these was Jabbo, a young black who had been on heroin six years. He had accepted Jesus during a rally at one of the local high schools. After that he followed us everywhere. He would sit in the back of the meetings praising God and raising his hands in the air. One night we were invited to a large white church in the suburbs and we asked Jabbo to go along with us and tell what had happened to him.

That was a mistake. Jabbo was black, very black. The minute we walked in the church I could feel the tension. We had brought white former addicts to this same church and although they were dirty and ragged, they were accepted with joy. But Jabbo, even though he was clean and dressed in a new suit, was rejected. Nobody said anything, at least not to his face, but you could feel it all around you. And I felt it, too, because I was Jabbo's brother, not only in race but in the Spirit.

The rejection hurt especially since it came from God's people. During the next two months we were in Washington I felt it more and more. A lot of the whites, though they didn't cut me like they did Jabbo, didn't know what to do with me either. The only blacks they knew played football, or baseball, or were entertainers of some kind. I was simply a dope addict that had been saved. I didn't know how to play the piano, or sing, or talk intelligently about

Willie Mays or Wilt Chamberlain. And since I wasn't acceptable on a social level, we had nothing in common to talk about.

One night some of us were invited to dinner in one of the white suburbs. We were sitting in the den watching the early news before dinner when a picture of Rap Brown flashed on the screen. Rap was making the scene at the time and some of his preachments were revolutionary. The host slammed his hand on the table. "What do these niggers think they're doing?"

Before I knew it I was saying, softly yet deliberately, "Sir, I'm a nigger too."

I could see the color rising in his face as he looked around the room for help. But the other members of the Teen Challenge team, who felt the same way I did, were letting him handle it alone. Finally he cleared his throat and said, "Aaron, you're different."

"No, I'm not different. I'm a nigger."

I wasn't going to let the point drop. "If it wasn't for Jesus I'd be just another angry black out there saying we ought to kill whitey and bomb his buildings."

"That's what I meant," the man said uneasily, looking toward the kitchen and hoping for a call to dinner. "You're not a revolutionary."

"But I am, man. I am a revolutionary, out to change things. In Jesus' way, yes, but change things just the same."

The first day back in New York I went to see Sister Neal. Her face was sober as she poured me a cup of coffee. "There's something I got to tell you," she said. "I hope you'll forgive me."

"What's that?" I said, wondering, after all she had

done for me, how she could possibly ask me to forgive her.

"I've knowed where your Aunt Rose has been all
this time."

"What? But why didn't you tell me?"

"Because I was tryin to protect her. She's a proud
woman, Aaron. She's worked hard and she set a lot
of stock on you. I didn't want to get her hopes up and
see her let down again."

I was silent. I understood only too well.

"But now I'm satisfied this change is for keeps."

Aunt Rose, Sister Neal said, was living at a place
called Livingston Manor up in the Catskills. She had
bought a summer-resort hotel and was running it herself, with Uncle Arthur's help.

I borrowed a car and drove up. But the visit was
not what I had hoped for. It was strained and awk-
ward, with me doing most of the talking and Aunt
Rose sitting and listening. I finally finished my speech
and waited.

"I'm sorry, Aaron," she said quietly. "I want to believe you, I really do. I guess I just don't dare, yet."

I started to answer, then realized that only time,
not words—certainly not my words—could tell her
what she needed to know.

"I guess if you weren't quite so enthusiastic I could
find it easier to believe," she went on. "But all this
talk about Jesus, and the Holy Spirit, and miracles,
and healings—it's too much. I'm glad you say you're
off dope, and I believe you are. But it's like I'm sitting here listening to a stranger."

"Yes I know, Aunt Rose," I said.

"You see, I found out about your life, Aaron. Not
everything, probably, but more than I wish I knew.
Things I can't forget. Things that make me sorry I
had anything to do with giving you a start. Now you

expect me to believe that you're going to Bible College and become a preacher? It's just too much, Aaron."

She squared her thin shoulders in the brave little gesture I knew so well. "We're doing all right up here, Arthur and me. We're doing just fine. Isn't it strange?" she added. "I used to pray so hard I'd hear you say the very things you've said today. And now that I hear them, I can't believe."

She looked down at her hands folded so still on her lap. "I guess when you pray, you better be sure you can stand still for a miracle."

It was clear that Aunt Rose was still bound by the past. And a few days later I realized how far from free I was myself. Walking from the subway to Mrs. Neal's apartment I heard a truck backfire. Without thinking I began to run.

In my little room, still shaking, I remembered something Rat had said, about going to the top. Why shouldn't I do it? What did I have to lose?

Next afternoon I went to a phone booth in the back of a Brooklyn bar. Dropping a dime I dialed the almost forgotten number.

"This is Youngblood," I said when a voice answered. "You got a number for me."

There was a long pause and then the voice said. "Yeah." He gave me a number and I dropped another dime in the phone and dialed.

"This is Youngblood. I want to talk to Gino."

"I don't know no Youngblood," the new voice replied.

"The hell you don't," I exploded, feeling suddenly I was fighting for my life. "Put me through to Gino."

There was another long pause while I heard a hand

go over the mouthpiece and mumble of voices. Finally the voice said, "What's your number?"

I gave him the number of the phone I was calling from and hung up. Ten minutes passed while I sat in the hot booth, sweating and praying. Then the phone rang. The voice gave me the name of a restaurant off Times Square. "Be there at five tomorrow afternoon." The phone clicked dead.

I realized I could have just set myself up for an ambush. But they'd have no trouble killing me, in any case, and this might be my chance to live.

I was standing outside the restaurant when that same limousine pulled up and Gino stepped out. It had been more than a year since I had seen him but he acted like it was yesterday. He put his arm around my shoulder. "Let's go inside, Youngblood. We can talk there."

He took a table on the far side of the room, ordered espresso for two, and fanned himself with his paper. "This heat is killing me."

"Man, that's what I gotta talk to you about. The heat your guys are putting on me is about to kill me, too."

"Now Youngblood, you know it's nothing personal. Strictly a business matter."

"Man, would I try to hurt your business? It would be like committing suicide."

"We've heard you were doing a lot of talking."

"Sure man. I'm talking about Jesus Christ. I'm not talking about the business. I'm not even thinking about it. I haven't touched dope in six months."

"Aw, Blood. I can't believe that. Nobody comes off the stuff like that."

"Well, it's true. Look at me. I'm healthy. I'm fat. Man, I feel great! I've found God I tell you! Jesus has changed me."

He looked at me and wrinkled his forehead. "If you've come off dope you're the first one I know who's done it. But I hear you're going around preaching about the profits white drug dealers are taking from black people."

"I don't deny it man. I've been talking about all kinds of ways whitey's been putting down the black man. But I ain't been using no names. I don't know any names. You oughta know that."

He sipped his coffee. "You know, my wife and kids go to church. A man's a fool not be be on God's side. Just last week I gave the church a little bit of money so they could build a recreation center for the neighborhood. You know, keep the kids off the streets."

"Then you know what I'm talking about," I said, grasping. 'You know Jesus can change guys like me."

"I don't know anything about changing." His words were cool.

In contrast, my voice was shaking. "Listen man, have this contract pulled! I'm no threat to you in any way."

He pulled a pen from his coat pocket and began doodling on the edge of the newspaper. "What are your plans for the future?" he said.

I thought for a moment, realizing suddenly that I didn't have any. Like I had as long as I could remember, I was still living on a day to day basis. If there was going to be a street meeting I went along. If I heard of a meeting in a black church I'd go and might be asked to speak. My life had been totally reversed, but in the area of thinking about the future I was still back on the streets. Unknowingly this Mafia agent was forcing me to do something I knew God had wanted me to do for a long time, and that was to commit myself to a plan.

I began to pray silently in the Spirit, deep inside

me I could hear the joyful sounds tumbling over each other. Gino looked up from his doodling. "Well?"

Before my mind flashed a picture of that application Bishop Clemmons had handed by for the Bible School in Alberta. Was this what God wanted me to do?

"I'm ... I'm going into the ministry," I blurted out.

"The ministry? You mean you're going to be a priest?"

"I'm going to attend a school, a Bible School, in Canada," I said with growing assurance, "so I can learn Scripture and teach black people about Jesus."

The Holy Spirit was flooding me with peace, confidence, authority. "I intend to help my people. I intend to work in the black ghetto. I want to work for poor people, in some church where they can't afford to pay a salary. I want to help kids, kids on dope like the ones I hurt. I want to spend my life serving Jesus Christ."

The shaking was gone as I finished speaking. Never, never had I dreamed of such a purpose for my life. It had just come streaming out as I had opened my mouth.

Gino was still doodling on the margin of the newspaper. "Well," he said, clicking the button on his pen and returning it to his coat pocket. "I'll see what can be done." He stood up to leave and I stood up too. "Somehow, Youngblood, I envy you." He paused. "Maybe ..." But he cut himself off, nodded, and in a moment had walked from the restaurant.

I sat back down at the table. Crying. Thanking God. Overcome with the power that had not only give me courage but a shining new direction for my life.

Then I noticed it. The newspaper he had been doodling on. I picked it up and saw in the margin a drawing of a church. It was a neat little church with a cross on the roof, and from both sides came little stick figures of people. All around the edge of the page they came, walking, running—every one of them heading for that building with the cross up on top.

EPILOGUE—JAMIE BUCKINGHAM

WAS IT REAL?

ITS BEEN almost six years since that tension-filled summer afternoon when Aaron walked away from that Times Square restaurant. But these years have proved his conversion to be real.

First there was Bible College in Edmonton, Alberta, where, incredibly, he made the dean's list the second semester. Then, after hearing him preach, the school officials appointed him one of the school's traveling evangelists. It was on one of these preaching trips that he met and fell in love with Debbi Wallace, the beautiful daughter of a black pastor in Portland, Oregon. Following their marriage, Aaron became an associate minister in a local church. Later, he and Debbi opened, and moved into, a drug rehabilitation center which has reached thousands of young drug addicts on the west coast. Recently, his ministry has assumed national prominence with appearances on syndicated radio and television shows, plus speaking engagements in every major city in America.

Is this just another game? Is the new Aaron capitalizing on Youngblood's lurid past with a new hustle under the safe cloak of religion? Aaron's life speaks for itself. He has totally rejected any temptation to

profane the name of Jesus with his old hustling techniques in order to make a fast buck. Equally determined not to become a religious Uncle Tom, he has
limited his ministry to mostly poor blacks, and nearly
always in the ghetto.

Besides wanting to live a pure life, Aaron's most
searing passion is to tell his former associates about
Jesus. Of course he began with Rat, who is now in
full-time Christian ministry. Then, after leaving Bible
school, he sought out his mother and the rest of his
family. Just before this book went to the printer, it
was discovered that Aaron had led some of them to
accept Jesus as their personal Savior. Even Aunt
Rose and Uncle Arthur now acknowledge the change
in Aaron's life to be genuine.

But what of the others? It has not been all victory.

Barbara, following an abortion, returned to prostitution on the streets—outlawing, working without a
pimp. Her former beauty now gone and her body
racked with VD, she was last seen among that miser-
able army of street whores who turn ten-dollar tricks
in flea-bag hotels around Times Square.

Swinger died of an overdose.

Cadillac Walter died of an overdose.

Gino, the controller, was shotgunned to death while
eating lunch in a secluded Brooklyn restaurant. His
murder remains unsolved.

Although Aaron has been back into Harlem many
times, witnessing to his former friends, there remains
one last contact which still eludes him. The memory
of what he did to Toni continues to haunt him, much
as the memory of the stoning of St. Stephen remained
with the Apostle Paul. All Aaron knows is that following her relase from prison, she changed her name and
moved to another city. So the search continues. And
even now, when an invitation to preach comes from

some big city ghetto, Aaron and Debbi often stay on for an extra day. Sometimes he walks the streets at night, his eyes searching the faces in the crowds. One day, he believes, Toni will turn a corner in front of him and her eyes will look deep into his cleansed soul. Then, he prays, she, too, will come to know the Jesus who lives within, the Jesus who saves.